RIPE MANGOES

MIRACLE MISSIONARY STORIES FROM BANGLADESH

RIPE MANGOES

MIRACLE MISSIONARY STORIES FROM BANGLADESH

by Jay Walsh
with Patricia C. Oviatt
Foreword by Viggo Olsen, M.D.

REGULAR BAPTIST PRESS
1300 North Meacham Road
Post Office Box 95500
Schaumburg, Illinois 60195

Patricia C. Oviatt is a pastor's wife, mother and free-lance writer, living in Argos, Indiana. She is a graduate of Baptist Bible College of Pennsylvania and has written extensively for Regular Baptist Press.

Library of Congress Cataloging in Publication Data

Walsh, Jay, 1932-
    Ripe mangoes.

    1. Converts, Baptist—Bangladesh—Biography. 2. Missions—Bangladesh. 3. Bangladesh—Biography. 4. Bangladesh—Church history. I. Oviatt, Patricia C., 1928-   joint author. II. Title.
BX6493.W34   248'.246   78-8671
ISBN O-87227-060-2

© 1978
Regular Baptist Press
Schaumburg, Illinois
Printed in the U.S.A.
All rights reserved

DEDICATION

To my colleagues in Bangladesh whose lives and ministries have made the telling of these stories possible.

CONTENTS

Foreword by Viggo B. Olsen   9
Preface   11
1/ Kokha Sen: A pocketful of stones   15
2/ Oncherai Tipperah:
    Apostle Paul of the Tipperahs   23
3/ Shudhir Kanti Barua:
    A saint already crowned   35
4/ Debindra Das: Laundryman for the Lord   43
5/ Shabitri Barua: First Christian wedding   51
6/ Syeed Ul Hoq: Dare to be a Daniel   59
7/ Shukie Bahadur: Call me Happy   71
8/ Indra Boshone:
    Growing pineapples for the Lord   79
9/ Robindra Barua: Saved twice   87
10/ Robichandro Tipperah:
     Evangelist with a vision   95
11/ Ponindra Lal Barua:
     Dry shrimp and chili peppers   107
12/ Debapriya Roy:
     Out of the maze, into the light   115
Epilogue   123
Maps   126, 127

FOREWORD

FROM TIME IMMEMORIAL ripe mangoes have been a delicacy to the poetic and volatile inhabitants of the Ganges delta country, Bangladesh. Now *Ripe Mangoes* are served up in refreshing style to Americans and other English-speaking peoples. These delicacies, however, are the vibrant human fruits of missionary effort in "golden Bengal."

Each story details the life experience of a Bangladeshi who decided to follow the One Who so stirringly declared, "I am the light of the world; he who follows Me shall not walk in the darkness, but shall have the light of life" (John 8:12, NASB). From Hinduism, from Buddhism, from many walks of life they came into that light. Missionaries, dreams, a dank jail cell, Bengali Christians, calamities, and other unique happenings all played their part in these dynamic conversions. These mini-biographies will delight you and will serve as vivid illustrative material for those who teach and preach.

The author of *Ripe Mangoes* is a close personal friend whose life and testimony I greatly appreciate. Jay Walsh is not only a capable leader, but also he is a missionary who deeply loves the Bengali people and who, in turn, is loved by them. He does not here write about theory and academic matters. Rather, out of his background of rich experience, he tells us of flesh and blood people whose laughter ripples like the wavelets on a thousand Bangladeshi rivers, and whose tears pour forth as tumultuously as monsoon rains from leaden skies.

Viggo B. Olsen, M.D.

PREFACE

IT'S MANGO HARVESTTIME in Bangladesh! Spread across the tropical landscape, the large mango trees produce one of that land's sweetest fruits. Countless Bengali children (and missionaries too!) eagerly wait for those first mangoes to turn from hard green to soft yellow. Delicious, ripe mangoes!

The work of missions reminds me of mango picking. First one, then another. And soon thereafter is a large, sweet, abundant harvest! Missions is not winning the millions. It is winning the ones and twos . . . those whose hearts have been touched after weeks and months of patient, faithful witnessing.

We missionaries are sometimes prone to impress people in North America with statistics. We tell of the 84 million people in Bangladesh, living in a land whose 58,000 square miles is comparable to the State of Florida. (Florida's population is under 7 million!) Yet it is from among the nameless masses that we "harvest" precious souls whose lives are gloriously changed by the living Word of God. No, not the millions, but the ones and twos.

It was that way with our Lord. The Son of Man, Who came seeking lost sinners, lived thirty-three years before He was crucified by them. At His ascension, 120 devout believers obediently gathered in Jerusalem to wait for the promised Holy Spirit. Incredible! Only 120 disciples after His years of effort? Yes.

Jesus began His earthly ministry by choosing twelve men who dared to follow Him. Around that select group, our Lord laid the foundation for the Church that was to come. In preparation for that time, He spent countless hours teaching, exhorting and rebuking those He had called to carry the gospel message to future generations.

Missionary work is no different today. Indeed, our ultimate goal is to reach the millions, but our immediate task is to lay a foundation. We gather a nucleus of believers, patiently teach them and pray that they will reach their own nation.

The Association of Baptists for World Evangelism (ABWE) began its pioneer evangelism in Bangladesh in 1956 when the country was still known as East Pakistan. In the succeeding years the cost of planting indigenous churches has been great. Three missionaries have laid down their lives in that land,* not to mention the multiplied thousands of dollars required to maintain an active missionary force. But slowly we are gathering fruit, fruit that will remain!

I shall never forget when we joined the missionary team. It was an exciting moment in March 1960 when a Greek freighter, the *Hellenic Splendor*, sailed to its mooring at jetty No. 17 in the teeming seaport city of Chittagong, Bangladesh.

There on the jetty, eagerly watching us come in, were the Miller and Barnard families. These stalwarts, who had pioneered the work of ABWE's Bangladesh field, stood in the sweltering midday sun waving white handkerchiefs, welcoming us to the land of our calling. We were thrilled indeed to be joining them as co-laborers in the work of God. We were also keenly aware as we looked at our awaiting friends that in recent months both families had suffered the loss of precious loved ones.

Mary Barnard was first. This lovely twelve-year-old girl had recently been operated on in India for appendicitis. But she still complained of pains in her side. She was sitting at the portable pump organ, playing and singing hymns of praise to the Savior she loved. Then, quite suddenly and very unexpectedly, her side began to ache. Before her parents could find help, she went Home to be with her Savior.

More recently, at the jungle station called Hebron, Helen Miller with her four small children, waved good-bye to her husband, Paul, as he left for the city of Chittagong to care for mission business. The little group stood on the riverbank and watched him disappear around the bend in the river. That happy family never saw their husband and father again. When Paul arrived in Chittagong, he complained of feeling ill. The following day he was subdued by a burning fever and paralysis. Efforts to get medical care proved futile. He, too, departed to be with his Lord and was buried the same day due to the oppressively hot climate. (These untimely deaths and

---

*Mary Barnard, Paul Miller, Harry Goehring

the great medical needs of the people led ABWE to establish the medical work in Bangladesh.)

In spite of these tragic experiences, the two families welcomed us to Bangladesh with genuine joy, taking us to their homes in Chittagong. We shared our experiences long into the balmy night.

Several days after our arrival, the Millers and Barnards drove us to the outskirts of the city, to the European cemetery, to view the graves of Mary and Paul. As we approached the freshly-placed markers, a holy hush fell upon us. We joined hands in a circle around the graves. A few silent, tear-filled moments passed. Then Mr. Barnard's steady, courageous voice broke the silence. "Let's pray together."

Our heads dropped instantly as he began a prayer I shall never forget.

"Our gracious, loving and merciful Heavenly Father, we stand here today around the graves of these Thy precious children. Our hearts ache, O Lord, because they are gone from us; but we rejoice in the knowledge that they are now in Your presence. O Lord, You know of the silent tears that have stained our pillows and the terrible emptiness in our hearts. Yet, O Heavenly Father, again today we commit it all to Thee. You said in Your Holy Word that unless a corn of wheat fall into the earth and *die*, it abideth alone and will not bring forth fruit. Precious Lord, bring forth from the lives of these Thy servants *much fruit* in this great and spiritually darkened land. Keep us also faithful to You until that day when we shall meet Thee face to face. Amen."

As it was during our Lord's earthly ministry, we, too, have found it a slow and plodding work to lay the foundation of an indigenous church in Bangladesh. However the lives of Mary Barnard, Paul Miller, and later, Harry Goehring, were not in vain. God *has* given fruit! An indigenous church *has* taken firm root. As ABWE missionaries laboring in Bangladesh, we are confident that there will yet be a more abundant harvest.

The following collection of stories tells of the miracles the grace of God is performing in Bangladesh. These believers represent but a few who have come to be a part of the growing church in that developing land.

Jay Walsh

Bringing forth precious fruit
(Vandals destroyed Mary Barnard's gravestone)

1
KOKHA SEN
A pocketful of stones

HE STOOD QUIETLY, giving the outward appearance of courage and assurance. The noisy, disorderly crowd jostled against him, jabbering, muttering and scheming. The air was tense, and Kokha Sen felt his scalp tingle. The tall, thin man stood with feet astride, hands in his pockets, fingering the rough stones he had scooped up and dumped there. A pocketful of stones!

He despised himself. Outwardly he looked confident, but inwardly he felt like a cringing coward. Any second now they would be alerted. When the planned signal was given by those in charge, he would . . . he would . . . or would he?

The hot, oppressive sun had sunk into the Bay of Bengal, and the refreshingly cooler evening breezes brought out many people. Chittagong, Bangladesh, was a busy city in the summer evening. Thousands of weary Bengalis poured into the narrow streets to relax, to shop and to enjoy the cooling breezes. Kokha Sen was one of them.

He hardly knew why he was here, scheming with this angry, threatening crowd. He knew why the *others* had come. They were here for a purpose.

The mission house with its spacious courtyard sat recessed off a busy street. Missionaries Victor Barnard and Gene Gurganus were preparing for the evening evangelistic meeting. They checked out the public address system and attended to the last-minute details.

The large courtyard in front of the yellow plastered building was rapidly filling with potential listeners. Bengalis were naturally curious about what the Christian missionaries would say. Soon the open-air meeting would begin.

Some of the crowd had attended previous meetings. They knew what the missionaries had been preaching. At all costs, they hoped to silence that powerful message! The informal congregation would be composed of Muslims, Hindus and Buddhists. All these people might be affected by the Christian message. Night after night some of them returned to hear the message.

The zealous priests had recognized and feared the power of the gospel. They were afraid that some of their number would become followers of Christ. Tonight these religious fanatics would try to silence the missionaries and their message by violence.

Kokha's fingers rubbed the rough texture of the stones in

his pocket. "Why am I here?" he asked himself. He felt distressed and miserable. Secretly he rebelled against participating in this prearranged harassment of the missionaries.

Kokha, a quiet, self-effacing man, had descended from a respectable high-caste Hindu family. His wife and two small daughters were still living in a Hindu village several miles up the Karnaphuli River from Chittagong. As a high-caste Hindu, he was obligated to perform numerous religious duties—daily burning of incense and preparing offerings for himself and his family. Day after day he mechanically went through the motions of his religion, not out of devotion to the Hindu gods, but out of obedience to ancient rites and to please his family. The religious observances did not relieve or fill the emptiness in his heart. His dissatisfaction grew daily.

Eventually he became tired of village life and bored with the tedious routine. Kokha began seeking for something of value and permanence. Perhaps, he thought, he could find peace of heart and soul in the city. Restless and dissatisfied, he arrived in Chittagong.

At least in Chittagong he did not have to keep up the meaningless pretense in his religion. He could avoid doing his *puja* (worship) without being seen by his family. Many are the seeking souls who have found anonymity in the crowded cities! Kokha was one of them.

Near the mission house on a dusty side lane was a row of bamboo furniture shops. Kokha secured work there as a carpenter's helper. The days were long, sultry and weary; but in the evenings he would wander about, listening to various street lectures. Sometimes he attended a cinema. These activities kept him from facing the void in his life.

One evening he came in contact with a Communist underground group. Their leader befriended him and urged him to attend their cell meetings. Their superficial enthusiasm was contagious, and for a time Kokha Sen thought maybe he had found reality. But as he learned more about their doctrine and tactics, he became sickened by their violent activities.

However, Kokha soon discovered that while it was relatively easy to join such a radical group, it was not that simple to disassociate himself from it. One evening after announcing that he wasn't going to attend any more meetings, a few of his "friends" attacked him. A knife scar on his shoulder served as a permanent reminder that the Communists were a menacing, dangerous group. His future—if he had any—must be found in another ideology.

Tonight the crowd, fanned into violent action by angry priests, was scheming to stone the Christian missionaries as soon as they appeared on the balcony to start the service. Kokha had no quarrel with the missionaries. He did not understand why anyone would want to harm the people whose only crime was to preach about Jesus Christ and the Christian religion. However, the hostile crowd hemmed him in on all sides. If he neglected to pick up stones, he could be labeled as a Christian sympathizer. So he filled his pockets with stones.

For what seemed like an hour, the stones and bricks pelted the mission house. Fortunately, the missionaries had taken refuge behind barred doors in time and were unhurt. Eventually the police arrived at the scene, and the crowd melted away. They had relieved their frustrations.

Kokha sadly shuffled off to his hot little room. Never had he been so unhappy and ashamed. True, he had not actually thrown any stones, but he had gone through the motions to deceive those around him. He felt just as guilty in his heart as if he had stoned the missionaries.

There was no sleep for him that night, or for the next two nights. His troubled mind kept reviewing the events of recent days. Finally he could stand it no longer. Stealthily he made his way to the back entrance of the mission house. His timid knock was answered by the same missionary his group had unsuccessfully tried to stone a few nights before! Missionary Victor Barnard greeted Kokha warmly, inviting him inside. Hot tea and cookies were served as the two men became acquainted. For the first time in his life, Kokha felt his cold heart softening. He was ready to listen.

The missionary got directly to the point. "Why have you come?" he asked. Kokha unburdened his soul, revealing his compelling desire to find peace with God. After carefully explaining the gospel story of Christ's love for sinners, the missionary led Kokha in a prayer of confession of sin and acceptance of Jesus as Lord and Savior.

As Kokha explained later, "My search for contentment was over. God's great peace filled the vacuum in my heart!"

He began regularly attending the missionary meetings. Soon he realized he had to tell his wife and children what happened. God would have it that way. But when he told his wife, she was decidedly unsympathetic. "Have you gone mad?" she angrily cried. Kokha had already been warned that he would have to suffer persecution for his stand. But he didn't think it would come from his wife and children!

"No matter what happens," he told them, "from now on, I am going to serve the Lord Who saved me and gave me peace."

Kokha returned to his job in Chittagong and continued fellowshiping with the Christian missionaries. As one of their very first believers, they all had plenty to learn together!

As months passed the missionary staff grew in size, making it possible to open a second mission station. Desiring to become involved in full-time Christian work, Kokha volunteered to help the missionaries. They located and purchased some land near the Chittagong Hill Tracts, eighty-five miles to the southeast. Here Hebron station was founded and dedicated to reach the primitive tribal people of the hills. Kokha was thrilled to be serving the Lord like the missionaries. The Hebron station was adjoined by a small Buddhist village. The local temple, in fact, was situated just across the fence.

It was January. The monsoon season was over. The village was buzzing with activity. This was the time when the annual *fanoosh* would be launched. Colorfully clad worshipers were coming and going from the temple where they presented their gifts to the priest in exchange for his blessings. The women of the village were busy in their bamboo huts preparing food for the evening banquet. The men and boys were making the *fanoosh*.

The *fanoosh* was a huge, inflatable paper balloon which they would set aloft at sundown as a climax to the day's religious activities. The bell-shaped paper balloon, when completed, would be nearly five feet high and three feet wide at the base. The launching of the *fanoosh* would not be an innocent kite-flying contest. It was a serious part of the idol worship. On this special day, called *Loki Purnima*, each Buddhist village in the land would send aloft their *fanoosh*. If it ascended above a certain altitude, the worshipers believed they would be assured of Buddha's blessing for another year.

Kokha, by now, was well-known to many of the people. He had many opportunities to befriend them. Even though they were skeptical and indifferent about his faith, Kokha was accepted and liked. "Are you coming tonight to watch us launch the *fanoosh*?" they invited.

Kokha wanted no part of their false worship, but he also looked upon this celebration as an opportunity to witness for his Lord and Savior. He carefully observed as the men and boys constructed the *fanoosh*. As they worked, they chanted.

"Speak, O Buddha,
Speak, O religion,
Speak, O priest, we pray.
For on the earth,
There's no such blessing,
As we'll receive today!"

He felt an overpowering sadness. He once had been in ignorance and darkness too. How he longed to prove to these dear people that *his* God was not a dead idol. His God was the only true God. He alone could bring peace, blessing and forgiveness of sin! He remembered the story of Elijah. Could he reenact that story for the people in Hebron? Certainly the God of Elijah was just as powerful today!

"I'll make a *fanoosh* too," he announced. "But my *fanoosh* will go higher and farther than yours."

Time was short, as the day was well gone. He hurried to the bazaar to buy colored paper, string and glue. Then he began making his *fanoosh* amid much jesting and laughter from the Buddhists. "Do you—a Christian—think your *fanoosh* can go higher than ours?" they challenged.

Kokha continued working while they watched and ridiculed. He put together the bamboo ribbing around which he glued the brightly colored paper. At last it looked like a giant bell. Next he suspended a ball of kerosene-soaked string like a pendulum through the center of the balloon, so that when it was aloft, it would dangle slightly below the craft. This would keep the *fanoosh* visible as it ascended into the night sky. After a few finishing touches, it was completed.

After sundown the Buddhists ate their feast and then prepared to launch their *fanoosh*. A smudge fire was started. When rich bellows of smoke poured forth, the *fanoosh* was held over the fire until it filled with smoke and heat. The ball of string was ignited, and the craft released. The village band gave the signal with trumpets. The priests began their incantations. The worshipers screamed and yodeled. The released *fanoosh* drifted lazily into the evening sky, visible only by the ball of burning string.

Now it was Kokha's turn. The people had heckled him because he was a Christian. They had been certain he would fail. They had laughed at his God. As Kokha launched his *fanoosh*, there was no band, no chants, no screaming and no noise. Only a mocking silence!

Courageously he filled the balloon with smoke and hot air. Then he lit the dangling ball of kerosene-soaked string. Slowly, lazily, the *fanoosh* ascended above the treetops, circled, then descended into the field!

Jeers and shouts of laughter greeted Kokha. The mocking crowd bellowed their taunts about his God! Kokha raised his hands to get the people's attention. "O people," he cried. "I know now the reason my *fanoosh* failed to rise. I forgot to PRAY. That is the most important part. My God, the true God, answers prayer!"

He recovered the *fanoosh* and rested his left hand on it. He raised his right hand to God in prayer. "Father in Heaven," he prayed while the silent crowd listened, "show these people that Christianity is the ONLY true religion by making my *fanoosh* go higher and farther than theirs. In Jesus' Name I pray. Amen."

Again the people gathered to watch him. Their silence spoke of unbelief. After he had made a few minor adjustments and relit the ball of string, Kokha released the balloon again. This time it did not falter. It rose rapidly into the night sky. The villagers watched in amazement as it soared to an unbelievable height. Not only had it passed theirs, but its light shone brighter than theirs had ever done.

The Buddhists stood with mouths gaped open, their heads lifted skyward in disbelief. An elated Kokha Sen made his way victoriously back to the mission compound. He had experienced his Mount Carmel. He had seen Elijah's God—and his—perform a miracle.

During Kokha's two years at Hebron, he had the joy of witnessing to many local people, several of whom came to know the Lord as Savior. Eventually, however, he returned to Chittagong and became part of the local church that was being formed there. He was also nearer his family, which had grown to include two boys. He longed to see his whole family come to know the Lord Jesus.

Then came the ugly Bangladesh war of 1971. The country was in turmoil. Hindu people everywhere were fleeing for safety as an angry Pakistan army blamed them for supporting the independence movement in the land. Some fled across the borders to India and Burma. Others took refuge in the jungle-covered hills. Still others were protected by compassionate friends.

Kokha came to missionary Reid Minich. He was nervous and upset. He explained the danger his family was in. His daughters might be discovered, taken away and raped. Reid was quick to understand Kokha's problem. He invited the Kokha Sen family to live with him in Chittagong until the danger was over. Kokha's four children came with their mother. She soon returned to the village home to look after the property. But the children stayed with Reid for nearly eight months until the civil war was over.

Reid fully realized what an opportunity he had. Daily devotions, songs, choruses and Scripture memorization became part of their daily lives. Reid was not only their protector, but their spiritual father too. Kokha was thrilled that his children were at last hearing about Jesus.

The war ended. Kokha's family returned to their village home. The struggle for independence had been used of God to bring a new spiritual dimension to this Hindu family. Only eternity will reveal what really happened in the lives of Kokha's children because of Reid's kind heart and faithful witness.

Today Kokha continues to serve his Lord and Master. He really believes that his whole family will one day, hopefully soon, join him in Christ. After all, even Elijah sometimes had to wait until his prayers were answered!

2
ONCHERAI TIPPERAH
Apostle Paul of the Tipperahs

HE WAS TIRED and thirsty. Still, his compelling love for Christ urged his weary feet along. Just ahead was a Mogh village. Maybe he could stop there for a drink of water. Evangelist Oncherai Tipperah was on a preaching tour in the Chittagong Hill Tracts along the Bangladesh-Burma border when he arrived at a Mogh tribal village. Mogh villages usually consist of eight to twenty bamboo houses perched on the ridge of a hill along a riverbank.

"Hello! Anybody here?" he called. The village seemed to be deserted. There was no answer, so he walked on and called again. This time an old Mogh tribesman peered out of a doorway and motioned Oncherai to come into his bamboo house. The houses are built on stilts with room underneath for the women's weaving machines and for cows, pigs and chickens to be housed. Scraps of food that fall through the bamboo floors are quickly gobbled up by the ground-level inhabitants!

Oncherai climbed up a notched log and greeted the old man, who was wearing a *loongie* (a long skirt tied at the waist). They sat down together on the veranda floor.

"Where is everybody?" the evangelist asked.

"Out working in the rice fields," the old tribesman replied. "They'll be back at sundown. They left me here to guard the village."

The Mogh people farm the mountainsides, as do the other tribes. Finding a lush jungle covered mountain, they'll slash down the undergrowth, let it dry for several weeks, then burn it. The ashes become the fertilizer for the rice seed that is planted over the burned area. The rice crop then springs to life when the monsoon rains begin in the spring.

Oncherai, hot and perspiring from walking in the midday sun, told the old man he was passing through his village. "I'm very thirsty," he said. "Could you give me a drink of water?"

The host disappeared to get a gourd of cool water. Meanwhile Oncherai glanced around the simple hut. A brazen statue of Buddha sat on an idol shelf above the door. His keen eyes also noted that fresh flowers and candles had recently been offered to the idol. When the old man returned with the water, he squatted in front of Oncherai.

"*Baba* [a respectful word meaning father]," Oncherai said as he took the water from the old man, "is that your god up there on the shelf?"

The wrinkled old man glanced up at his idol and nodded.

Oncherai pointed to the statue. "I see that your god has a mouth. How often does he talk with you?"

The tribesman's faded eyes gave a quick look at the idol. He shook his head. "He doesn't talk."

"He has eyes," Oncherai continued. "Can he wink them? Can he see you?"

A deliberate shake of the head was the only response.

"Well," Oncherai progressed, "if he can't talk and can't see, then surely he must be able to hear you. Has he ever smiled when you talked with him?"

By this time the old man was visibly irritated. "Of course not," he spat. "He's made out of brass."

"Who made your god?" Oncherai pursued.

"The brass smith over in Lama Bazar."

Oncherai zeroed in. "Baba, isn't the *maker* of a thing greater than the thing itself?" As the man reflected on this amazing proposition, Oncherai continued, "I know the brass smith in Lama Bazar. One day he cheated my wife on some bracelets he made. That man is a sinner! He's cheated many people. Yet you are telling me *he* made your god!"

The old Mogh gentleman hung his head as the truth of what Oncherai was saying sunk into his heart. Then Oncherai took the Bible from his cloth shoulder bag, opened it, and told the man about his Living Savior, the Lord Jesus Christ. "Jesus Christ can hear, speak, see and help. He isn't a dead, useless idol!"

Before he left the village that afternoon, Oncherai heard the old tribesman call upon the name of Jesus for salvation. A tear-stained, happy face beamed at him as he climbed down the notched log and went his way.

Oncherai recalls the time before he was truly saved. He had spent many years searching for peace. His Hindu parents lived in the northern quarter of the Chittagong Hill Tracts near the Indian border. Both of them were drinkers of rice whiskey and worshipers of Ram, a leading Hindu god. Oncherai remembers: "I would listen to my parents and the other villagers shouting, '*Hori, Ram! Hori, Ram!*' [Praise to Ram] for hours at a time. They would call until their voices grew hoarse. All the while they were getting more and more drunk, but Ram didn't answer them. I used to watch and listen closely, hoping Ram would shout back from the skies; but he never did."

Death is always a heartbreak. It was for Oncherai too. He

was only seventeen when his parents died after a smallpox epidemic swept the village. The bodies of his parents were placed on the funeral pyre, and the wailing and the incantations of the priests began. He shivered, watching the torch kindle the wood that would consume the dead bodies. His soul was tormented. Was there an afterlife? Did death end it all?

He decided, "Maybe education is the answer. Maybe if I learn to read and write, I will find answers for my heart."

Then Pastor Dala, an itinerant Indian evangelist, came to his village. For the first time, Oncherai heard the truth about the gospel. "Peace is found in a Person, Jesus Christ," he was told. "Unless you receive Him, you'll die in your sins!" Pastor Dala's words made a strong impression, but Oncherai made no decision at this time.

A few months later he married, and again sorrow came into his life. One year after the wedding, following the birth of his first son, his young wife died of malaria fever. The next few years he worked with a single purpose: to provide a living for his baby boy. Then at the age of twenty-five, he married again, this time the village headman's daughter.

During those years a spiritual battle raged in his heart. He forced himself to perform *puja* (worship) to Ram and Sita, two of Hinduism's chief gods. But something about the rituals caused him to rebel, especially since Pastor Dala had introduced him to the Lord Jesus Christ, the only One Who could forgive sin.

Oncherai learned about a Christian missionary who lived in the village of Chandraghona, nearly forty miles away. Early one morning he started out to find the "foreign missionary sahib." Maybe *he* would tell him more about this Jesus-person! Three days later he arrived at the missionary's house, only to be turned away by a gruff guard. But Oncherai wasn't to be sidetracked. He had traveled forty miles and wanted answers to his soul's questions. From a distance he waited until he saw the missionary leave his compound. He ran to catch up with him and started to talk. How he hoped to learn more about Jesus Christ!

But the missionary had too much on his mind to sense the visitor's unspoken need. He was too busy to sit and talk. He wasn't too busy, however, to sell Oncherai one of the Bengali New Testaments he carried in his shoulder bag. Thrilled with his purchase, Oncherai hurried back to his village, announcing, "I am now a Christian." But he was totally illiterate!

"Even though I couldn't read it, I felt I had an important book in my hands," Oncherai recalls sadly. "I was determined to be a Christian. Being a Christian couldn't be any worse than being what I had been: a Hindu!"

As a professing but ignorant "believer," Oncherai came in contact with another Christian from the adjoining Bawm tribe. Chala, his new friend, helped Oncherai learn more about the terms and practices of Christianity. Yet, as Oncherai discovered, Chala had many inconsistencies in his own life. He needed more teaching in Christian ethics and morals.

For five years Oncherai pretended to be a Christian. Then God used a series of dramatic events to lead this "seeker" to the truth—and to peace.

One day Chala came with exciting news. Missionaries had moved into the southern area of the Chittagong Hill Tracts near Lama Bazar. "We might get work at the new mission station," he told Oncherai. "Surely they'll want to hire us. We're both Christians." Early the next morning they began their trek. After three days of walking, climbing mountains and fording rivers, they finally reached their destination.

Victor Barnard, a veteran missionary, had pioneered the opening of the mission station which he named Hebron. The two men who came to him for jobs seemed to be genuine. He interviewed them and decided to hire them both. They would be interpreters and evangelists to assist him in tribal evangelism.

Recalling the days that Chala and he worked for the missionaries, Oncherai confessed, "Both of us were only there for the money. We really didn't have the least interest in spiritual things." To illustrate his confession, he related how they had cheated. "Chala and I did the marketing for Barnard Sahib. It was easy to make some extra cash. In fact we made it in two ways. As no receipts of purchase are given in the bazaar, we lied about the actual cost of a purchase, saying it cost three *takas* when it was only two. And we would charge for two pounds of meat when we had only bought one and a half pounds! We would then split the profit and use it to buy tea, sweets or tobacco for ourselves. We were both hypocrites!"

Eventually Chala left, but Oncherai moved his family nearer the Hebron station. Somehow he felt he needed to know more of the Christian message. Missionary Joyce Wingo, a tall, attractive Texan who had been trained in linguistics, began to use Oncherai as a language informant. Joyce and Mary Lou Brownell had come to replace the Barnards who left for furlough in America. Meanwhile Oncherai was learning to read and write.

We Walshes joined Joyce and Mary Lou at Hebron in the fall of 1960. Our ministry was to be tribal evangelism. Less than two weeks after we arrived, a brand-new eighteen-horsepower Evinrude outboard engine was stolen from us. We had stored the motor inside our first home. When we moved to a larger house nearby, we left the engine in the old building, under lock and key. But there is very little security in a house made of bamboo! The engine, which cost $250, was worth three times that much in Bangladesh. It was a gift from missionary Helen Miller, in memory of her late husband, Paul, to be used for our transportation needs up and down the Matamahari River on which Hebron station was located.

I was distressed. This was plainly a matter for the police. I sent a report to the officer in charge of our jurisdiction. Three days later, a police inspector and two constables arrived on foot. They began their inquiry with the mission employees. "This had to be an inside job," said the tough-looking inspector.

And he was right! After interrogating our maintenance man, a professing Bengali Christian, he confessed to the crime. He also (falsely) implicated some of the Tipperah men on the station. "Oncherai is also guilty," he cried. So he and two others were arrested. At this point the police called me. They had solved the case. I was stunned to see Oncherai lashed together by rope with the other men. The agonizing look on his face revealed his great physical pain as well as his embarrassment. "How could he be involved?" I asked myself.

But there on the ground at their feet lay the engine. It was still covered with mud. Shortly before, the police had recovered it from a dense thicket near the mission compound. It had been completely buried! The gruff inspector announced, "We are taking them to Cox's Bazar for trial. You will be called as a witness."

Me? A witness? What for? I was learning fast about legal procedures in my adopted land. I knew that Cox's Bazar was a small seacoast town on the Bay of Bengal. It was also the subdivision headquarters where criminals were tried and jailed. It was fifty long miles away—miles that would have to be covered by foot, by boat and by bus.

What would happen to Oncherai? Was he really guilty? A thousand questions filled my mind. I still was not fully conversant in the language, and so I felt the frustration all the more keenly. If only I could talk with Oncherai and learn the truth! With a broken heart I watched him being led away with the others, his head bowed in shame. This was a shattering experience for us missionaries. Joyce, especially, felt her world had collapsed. She needed Oncherai in her language work. We had all placed so much faith in him because of his seemingly genuine interest in the Christian faith. He had a natural talent for preaching that couldn't be denied. Now he was in prison!

"The jail was crowded and dirty," Oncherai related later. "More than forty of us were jammed into one small, dark room. Rats would come and nibble on us after darkness settled in. It was a terrible place!"

But it was in Cox's Bazar prison that GOD was finally able to arrest Oncherai! Until then he had been a Christian in name only, a hypocrite, a man whose stiff pride had yet to be broken.

"One night I dozed off to sleep while crouching in a corner," Oncherai remembered. "I dreamed a wonderful dream. It was as if an angel had descended from Heaven and spoke to me. [It is interesting to note that dreams often have real spiritual meaning to Christians in Bangladesh.] He smiled and said, 'Oncherai, don't weep any longer. You won't die in jail. God has much work for you to do.' "

When Oncherai awoke, he felt a warm surge of joy flood his being. With tears of joy and still crouching in his corner, he confessed his sins and asked Jesus Christ to save him. He had just experienced the forgiving power of the blood of Christ! Oncherai's conversion gave him a whole new outlook on life. He began to witness to the other men around him. The days didn't seem nearly as long as before.

Three months passed before his case was finally heard in court. The trial date was set and cancelled twice before it took place. Yet Oncherai was confident the Lord would not forsake him. I made the trip down river to Cox's Bazar. That terrible, dark night was one I'll never forget. A cyclonic storm lashed the coastline! I spent a sleepless night listening to gale winds and rain beat upon my quarters. I was to learn later that more than five thousand fishermen lost their lives on the two islands I could see from the rest house where I'd stayed!

The next day I was escorted to a simple brick building which was crowded with onlookers. (No doubt they had come to see me—not the criminals.) The accused were handcuffed to a policeman in a cell opposite the prosecuting officer. Oncherai was smiling. Standing in a walk-in lectern before the judge and under oath (British law still prevails in Bangladesh), I replied to the lawyer's queries.

I don't remember much about the questions, but I do remember the "lazy fan" that hung from the ceiling. In a town without electricity, somebody had dreamed up an ingenious cooling system to combat the hot, humid weather. A large, thick blanket was draped over a parallel hanging pole. A rope connected to it through a pulley system was jerked back and forth by a squatting male servant. This caused the blanket to flap, thus providing a "fan" for cooling the courtroom!

Later the same day, after the trial, the officer in charge told me confidentially that he was certain Oncherai had been falsely accused. Oncherai and his fellow tribesmen were set free that evening and joyfully accompanied me back to Hebron. So Oncherai was not a thief! He had been accused out of jealousy. He was free now, but very weak and covered with ugly sores. He returned to his village in the hills only to find that his wife was cold and indifferent to him. His neighbors also turned their backs on him, still believing he was a thief.

With an aching heart, Oncherai decided he had to clear himself. He called the entire village to a meeting. Fearlessly and unashamedly he proclaimed, "I am not guilty of stealing the mission speedboat engine. Yet I don't blame the missionaries for making a case with the police. They did what was right. The truth is, God punished me for being a hypocrite. I was a Christian in name only. God allowed me to suffer so He could show me His deep love."

The villagers listened as he continued, "In jail I came to really know my Savior and Lord. When you spank your children, you do so because you love them. You want them to grow up right. God had to spank me, too, because He loves me."

His wife and neighbors believed him, and at last there was reconciliation. Oncherai was truly saved.

From that day, Oncherai committed his life to serve God as an evangelist. Since his jail experience in 1960, he has learned to read the Bible. This valiant man has trekked hundreds of weary miles, preaching to his own people and to other tribal groups scattered in the hill country along the Bangladesh-Burma border. Because of his faithfulness to the Word in witnessing, hundreds have come into the Body of Christ. Today, mainly because of Oncherai's efforts, there are ninety Christian villages in the Hill Tracts!

One day, after an extended preaching tour, Oncherai returned to give me his exciting report. He told of the Satanic opposition and hardship he suffered in various villages he had visited. Then, pointing to the gold ring on my finger, he said, "Sahib, that ring first had to go through fire and be pounded, filed and buffed and polished before it became a shining circle of beauty. That's the way God is molding and shaping me until someday I may be found in Him without spot and blemish. In spite of many hardships, I know He is with me."

Occasionally Oncherai would run into problems he couldn't solve alone. Once he came to me with a delegation of Christian men from Chimpru village.

"Sahib," he explained, "two policemen are trying to extort one thousand *takas* [about $200] from Ramoni deacon. A false case has been made against him, and they'll drop it if he raises the money to pay them off. We need your help."

I had known Ramoni for many years. He had been chosen a deacon by his fellow Tipperah tribesmen several years before.

"What do you have to say?" I asked Ramoni.

Ramoni told me how his aged mother died when she slipped and fell from the high veranda on his house. Someone falsely reported to the police that he had pushed her! That "someone," who had recognized an opportunity to make some easy money, was cooperating with the unscrupulous officers. The officers were charging Ramoni with murder!

After listening to his story, I sat down and typed a letter to the officer in charge of their police station. Oncherai delivered it in person. In it I related the truth about the case and assured them I was prepared to testify on Ramoni's behalf. I never received a reply, but Ramoni's case was dropped; he was never bothered again. Oncherai was gratified that he could be involved in solving the problem.

For years I have been a spiritual father and teacher to Oncherai. Our Paul-Timothy relationship has been the highlight of my ministry in Bangladesh. Periodically he would come for Bible teaching. "Sahib," he would say, "I've been reading in the Book of James. There are so many sweet things there, but there's so much I don't understand. Could we go through that book together?"

So every day for a week, morning and afternoon, the two of us would sit together, feasting on the Word. Invariably during a session together his eyes would fill with tears, and he would say, "Oh, if only all my people could be sitting here just now. They could hear the same precious teaching that I'm hearing." And invariably I would reply, "Oncherai, that's not possible. God has richly blessed you. Now *you* go and preach what you've learned to your people."

After a week of filling his own soul, he would leave me and preach again in the villages. Because of his love for the Word and burden for his people, I have felt justified in referring to Oncherai as "the apostle Paul of the Tipperahs."

It has been my privilege over the years to teach him and help him. But I must confess that more often than not Oncherai has been *my* teacher! On numerous occasions I had the distinct impression that I was dealing with one of God's choicest servants.

Oncherai is now in his fifties. He is considered to be an old man by his people. There's no doubt that the rigors of jungle life have made him old before his time, but God has given him a fine family. Two of his sons are now studying the Bible. They plan to "take up the mantle" of their respected evangelist-father!

Oncherai and his sons

Dr. Robert T. Ketcham and Oncherai

3

SHUDHIR KANTI BARUA
A saint already crowned

WORD QUICKLY SPREAD throughout the hospital mission station at Malumghat. "Shudhir has been admitted to the intensive care unit and is not expected to live! Come! We'll have a special prayer meeting starting immediately at the evangelistic center."

This news about Shudhir didn't come as any great surprise to us missionaries. Shudhir Kanti Barua, a tall, extremely thin man with a sunken chest, probably had emphysema. Once he nearly died in a coughing spell. For many months we had been aware of his fragile health. Nevertheless it was thrilling to see the new Christians responding to the crisis by immediate, spontaneous, intercessory prayer. Shudhir was the respected, beloved leader of their yet-unorganized local church.

I first met Shudhir in 1960 when we moved to our interior mission station called Hebron. (Hebron was so named because it was a place where Biblical Abraham sojourned; a place of rest.) Bilchari Buddhist village was only a stone's throw from the mission compound. Only a few rice paddies separated our home from Shudhir's.

His house was a large mud duplex structure with a grass roof, now in run-down condition. Certainly at one time their family had seen better days. Shudhir was introduced to me as a new Christian, although he had not yet been baptized. (Baptism to the non-Christian Bengali is viewed as the act indicating full and final renunciation of the former religion.)

One day as we sat together on the riverbank, he related to me the history of his family. "We weren't always this poor, Sahib," he said proudly. "My father was a big *zamindar* [landowner] who had possession of over 100 acres of paddy land. We even had hired laborers working for us."

I could see tears form in Shudhir's eyes as he shared this information with me.

"After my father died in 1942, my mother became responsible for the land and for paying the taxes. She didn't understand much about legal matters, so we fell in arrears. One day we received a notice that our property had been confiscated by the government. Fearful and upset, my mother sent me with my uncle to check on the matter. There had to be some mistake! In the land office we learned that our property had not only been confiscated but had already been resold to a Muslim *zamindar!*"

This was a shattering experience to Shudhir and his mother. They had fallen from great wealth to great poverty in the matter of a few months. Later they learned that the loss of their property had been engineered by an unscrupulous land-grabbing Muslim, who paid a large sum of money to the land officials.

However, had this experience not taken place, Shudhir might never have come to know Christ. When the missionaries opened Hebron station at Bilchari in 1959, Shadhir, now in desperate need of employment, was hired as a day laborer to help clear the land. His wage was set at *takas* 2.5 per day (50¢), which was standard throughout the country at the time.

Shudhir's work as a simple *coolie* (laborer doing menial tasks) brought him into contact with missionaries Mr. and Mrs. Victor Barnard. For the first time in his life he learned about the Person of Jesus Christ!

As a child, Shudhir *almost* became a saffron-robed Buddhist priest. His father, a devoted Buddhist, built his own private temple where he performed his daily religious duties. These included placing daily offerings before the image of Buddha. Shudhir, his younger brother and two sisters, had to accompany him in these rituals.

"One day," Shudhir recalled, "my father had my head shaved bald and sent me to the largest Buddhist temple in our district. I was about twelve years old when I entered the monastery against my will. After nine days of intense indoctrination and fasting, I decided I wanted no more. I put up such a fuss and temper tantrum that the priests notified my father, who hurried to see what was wrong." He smiled wryly and continued, "The outcome was that my father had to pay the priests for my freedom and the inconvenience I had caused them. I was determined that whatever the cost, I would enjoy life—but not in a monastery!"

Shortly after this experience, Shudhir's father died from an attack of malaria, leaving him, as the oldest son, responsible for the family. And it was during this period that their land was snatched away.

Shudhir had attended school for five years before his father died. After that, he could not afford to continue. He was only sixteen when he married a village girl. A year later their son Benu was born. Although he was thin and sickly, Shudhir farmed a small plot of rented land and cared for several cows to help make a meager living. This was quite a change from the prosperous life he had enjoyed when his father was alive.

During all those years, he only heard about Christianity

once—a brief reference to Christ in a history book! But now, working for the missionaries, Shudhir was hearing plenty! Every evening after work, missionary Victor Barnard would gather his workers together and preach to them about Jesus. One day the missionary announced that he would have a special meeting. Over one hundred people came, including all the village men. After seating them on bamboo mats, he proceeded to explain why the Christian missionaries had come to Bilchari.

"None of us had heard much about Jesus Christ before," confessed Shudhir; "so we really didn't understand all he was saying. We listened politely because he had announced that tea and cookies would be served after the meeting. None of us wanted to miss that!" At the close of the meeting, the Barnards served the people and also distributed Christian tracts and booklets. Shudhir was to read and reread those tracts in the days to come!

Rumors of that meeting quickly spread to the Muslim village of Bilchari. The Muslims, being the majority community, were vociferous in their condemnation of the Buddhists for showing interest in Christianity. "You are going soft on your ancient principles," said one leader. (For whatever reason, many Muslims fear the advance of the Christian faith. They would rather the people remain Buddhists than convert to Christianity. That way there would be little threat to their religion.)

Shudhir remembers the leaders of his village calling a hurried meeting to discuss the accusations and taunts. "The missionary sahib will slowly make all of us into Christians," one man reasoned. "They will destroy our religion just like the Muslims are saying." By the time the meeting ended, they made up their minds that no Buddhists would show up for work the next day. They would put pressure on the missionaries to refrain from preaching.

The following day, the workmen did not appear. Missionary Barnard walked to the Buddhist village to find out why. He spotted a group of idle men standing outside Shudhir's house and asked, "What happened? Why didn't you come to work today?"

A spokesman answered defiantly, "We won't work for you anymore. If you preach to us about your Christian religion, you can just find somebody else to do your work."

Mr. Barnard replied, "All right. That's up to you. I am compelled to preach about Jesus Christ because God sent me here to do that! We also wanted to help you people financially by giving you work. But if you are not interested, then I'll hire others." He then turned and walked away.

Shudhir recalls, "He did just that! Barnard Sahib hired very willing Muslims and Hindus to work for him. Some were the same men who had put pressure on us, warning us about converting to Christianity! It turned out to be a very nasty, sly trick they had played on us."

When the Buddhists saw what happened, they regretted their hasty decision. But now what could they do?

Shudhir, however, continued his visits to the mission station where he listened with a receptive heart to the witness of the missionaries. Once the missionary gave an object lesson. He was explaining to Shudhir how Christ can relieve the burden of sin. "He picked up a large, heavy book and laid it on my hand," Shudhir remembered. "Then he asked me to lift my hand slowly. The book was very heavy. Then he took the book away and asked me to lift my hand again. Now it seemed light. Barnard Sahib said this is what happens when Jesus lifts the great burden of sin from our hearts. The logic of that illustration was what God used to convict me of my sin. I accepted Jesus as my personal Lord and Savior right then and there!"

Three years later, in 1963, against the wishes of his family and villagers, Shudhir obeyed the Lord in believer's baptism. Until that time he had delayed because of family pressure. But now he was willing to go all the way. He had counted the cost.

In 1968 he moved to Malumghat, home of the Memorial Christian Hospital, where he took charge of the newly established Bible Correspondence School. This ministry involved working with interested Bible students by mail. Advertising leaflets with return postcards would be distributed in a certain area. A few recipients would return the postcards, requesting to be enrolled as students. Shudhir then would mail out Gospels of John and sets of questions to be completed by the students. Once these were returned, he would correct the answers and forward a second set of questions. In this way a student completing five courses would earn a New Testament. Upon completion of the ten Bible courses, he would earn a complete Bible.

This ministry was well suited for Shudhir because of his

Group of Christians, missionary Gene Gurganus and Kokha Sen at Shudhir's baptism

frail health. He often dealt with students who would come to visit the Christian bookroom, helping them to understand more about Christ. During Shudhir's brief ministry, the Bible Correspondence School grew to over a thousand students representing all religions.

Although he was happy serving the Lord, Shudhir was also sad. When he first moved to the hospital to serve with us, his wife flatly refused to come. She was still a devout Buddhist. It was nearly two years before she was willing to move and live with her husband. We learned later that her strict father was to blame for her actions. Not long after joining her husband, she and the two oldest children accepted the Lord as Savior and were baptized. God had answered Shudhir's prayers.

He became the spiritual leader of a nucleus of believers who had come to know the Lord through the efforts of our medical/surgical evangelism. He acted as their pastor, preaching on Sunday mornings and leading the weekly prayer meetings. It was during those busy days that he suffered an attack of emphysema and was carried unconscious to the emergency room. While the doctors worked over him, the national believers prayed for his deliverance.

God heard those prayers. He performed a miracle for Shudhir and raised him back to health. (Or was it for the strengthening of the church?) After several weeks of convalescing, Shudhir took up his duties again. The Lord blessed his leadership, and the church continued to grow.

The political situation in the country at this time was shaky. A national election was planned for December 1970. The army rulers were at last going to submit to civilian rule. Winds of discontent were already blowing in the land. The Bengalis were seeking more political autonomy. The power of their popular leader, Sheikh Mujibur Rahman, was beginning to be felt and feared.

The thirst for freedom from their non-Bengali military masters led to open revolt in the early months of 1971, throwing the country into chaos. It affected all our missionaries; it also affected Shudhir.

Because of an angry advancing army, the evacuation of missionary personnel came as a very strong recommendation to us from the United States consul in the capital city of Dacca. The announcement to evacuate came over the Voice of America shortwave radio program and was picked up on the eleven P.M. news by nurse Becky Davey.

April 20, 1971, will always be remembered as the night we decided to cross over the border into Burma in obedience to the wishes of the U.S. State Department. With the evacuation of all missionary women and children, including the missionary nurses, it was also necessary to close the hospital. Doctors Ketcham and Olsen remained behind to watch over the hospital property. The day after we crossed into Burma, the doctors decided to evacuate the Bengali staff to the Hebron station, twenty miles in the interior east of Malumghat. Hebron would provide a safe haven for them.

Hebron was accessible by riverboat or by walking over jungle-covered mountains. A Bengali Christian reported, "It was a long, hard trip from Malumghat to Hebron for us all. We had to travel by foot most of the way. It was extremely difficult for Shudhir, who was still very weak."

The evening they arrived at Hebron, Shudhir enjoyed a delicious meal on the veranda of his village home. His aged mother had prepared a special chicken curry for her firstborn son, who hadn't been home for a year. When his meal was finished, Shudhir began to cough. Then he choked. No one could help him. God quickly released this beloved brother from his pain, and he was absent from the body and most assuredly at Home with his Lord. There was great sorrow in the camp that night.

Early the next morning the Christians lovingly carried their dear leader's body to a corner of the mission compound and tenderly laid it to rest. Under normal conditions, probably only one or two Christians would have been around to attend Shudhir's funeral. But now, because of the evacuation, almost the entire church was gathered there, apart from any American missionaries, to honor their beloved brother. They sang hymns, prayed, and departed, knowing that Shudhir's condition was much better than theirs. His coronation day had arrived. He was now a saint in the presence of his Lord!

4

DEBINDRA DAS
Laundryman for the Lord

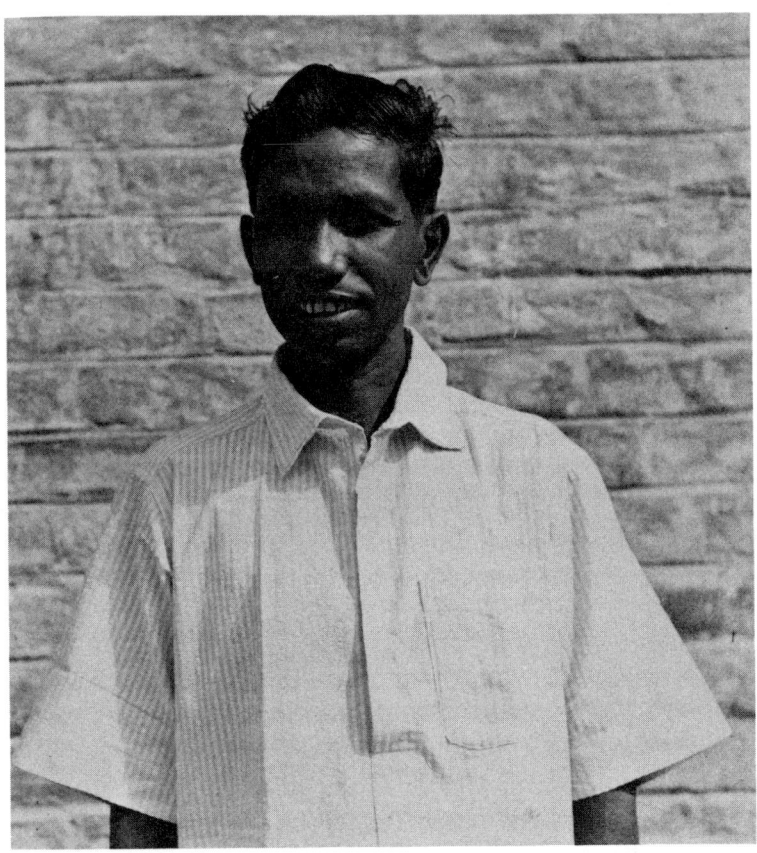

HARRY GOEHRING, our beloved friend and co-laborer, was dead! All of us were shocked and saddened by the untimely death of the 32-year-old missionary who went to be with the Lord on June 16, 1965. Overwhelmed with sadness, we gathered in Dr. Vic Olsen's apartment to pray and ask God to comfort the hearts of Nancy and the children.

While we prayed and made arrangements for the funeral, a little man quietly led his wife into the room where Harry's body lay, covered with a sheet. "I was there," Debindra Das, our tiny laundryman, said. "I was ironing the clothes in that hallway. I could see Goehring Sahib through the open door. I watched his face. I watched him die!" Debindra drew his wife closer. "Goehring Sahib died peacefully!" He leaned over the bed and pulled back the coverlet. "Look at his face," he told his wife Promilla. "See for yourself how peaceful he looks!"

The laundryman's wife gazed into the serene face of the missionary who was now in the presence of the Lord. "Yes," she admitted as if to herself, "I see it. He really does look happy!"

"See?" Debindra announced triumphantly, "this is what it is like for a Christian to die. It's a peaceful, happy experience for them. Not like when Hindus die. You know how our people die—fearing death, fighting it, frothing at the mouth, trying to avoid it. Then there's wailing and uncontrolled weeping among those who still are living!"

While the missionaries were praying, God used Debindra Das to bring forth the *firstfruits* of Harry's death. Promilla, Debindra's wife, accepted the Lord as her personal Savior that very night!

The first time I met Debindra was in 1960 on a trail leading from the Hebron station to Lama Bazar. We met in the middle of the rice paddies. He was returning from the bazaar, heading home. A bundle of beautifully clean white shirts over his arm caught my eye.

"Where did you get those shirts?" I asked, fingering one of them.

"They belong to different people," he replied. "I'm a *dhopa* [laundryman], and I'm delivering these shirts now." (Not only did the *dhopa* have to pick up the dirty shirts from his customers, he also had to deliver the freshly laundered shirts if he expected to keep his business prospering.)

As we talked, I learned that he was a low-caste Hindu who lived in a refugee village across the Matamahari River from the mission station. (The government had relocated a large group of people there a few months before.) It was obvious that Debindra, a tiny 4' 10" man, had a serious speech impediment. He stammered terribly as he talked with me.

"Would you be willing to do our laundry?" I asked him. "I really need to hire someone to help my wife on washdays twice a week." As an enticement, I told him about our gasoline-powered Maytag washing machine which would get shirts even whiter than his method. He had to beat the dirt from clothes on a log in the river, then soak them in bluing. Finally, he would spread them on the grass to dry in the bright sunshine.

His curiosity was aroused. "Sahib," he said, "I'll come to your house in the morning. I want to see the machine you're talking about. I've never heard of such a thing before!"

Sure enough, Debindra was there on our veranda when we arose. He cleared his throat several times to let us know he was present. We invited him in and served him tea and cookies (common Bengali courtesy). Then Eleanor tossed a load of white clothes into the washer. With a quick jerk of the rope, I started the machine and watched Debindra's face.

His eyes widened as he observed the agitator doing the job he had to do by hand. It was like magic to him! After such a dramatic demonstration, Debindra was more than willing to become our laundryman. He just *had* to learn how to operate that machine! It took a few experiences, however, before he was able to get the clothes through the wringer without popping off all the buttons! But it wasn't long before he conquered the Maytag and even proudly demonstrated his skill to his friends as he worked!

One washday Debindra failed to show up for work. He didn't even send us any word as to the reason. Eleanor did the washing alone. We were very concerned, wondering if he were sick, or if we had unknowingly offended him. Finally he came, stammering sadly that he no longer dared work for us. Sad-faced and stooped-shouldered, tiny Debindra said, "My firstborn daughter died in the night. I couldn't come to work because of the burial ceremony in the morning. But the real reason I'm quitting is because the priests told me my little girl died as a punishment by the evil spirits. They said the spirits are angry because I am working for you Christians!"

Eleanor and I expressed our sorrow over his daughter's

death. "Debindra," I said, "please believe us. Your daughter died because of the fever, not because you are working for us. What the priests are telling you is simply not true."

We sat together on the veranda, and I explained to him the simple gospel message of God's love and the meaning of death. He listened politely. When I finished, I challenged him to accept Christ's offer of free salvation. "Jesus can wash away your sins and make your life whiter than any clothes you can wash," I told him. "He will also bring peace to your troubled mind."

I opened the Bible and read Isaiah 1:16-18: "Wash you, make you clean; put away the evil of your doings from before mine eyes; cease to do evil; Learn to do well; seek judgment, relieve the oppressed, judge the fatherless, plead for the widow. Come now, and let us reason together, saith the LORD: though your sins be as scarlet, they shall be as white as snow; though they be red like crimson, they shall be as wool."

Debindra listened to the Word of God intently. "I'll think about it, Sahib," he promised. As he walked away, I encouraged him to reconsider his decision and come back to work.

The next washday he reported for duty. We were so happy that he had decided not to follow the priests' advice.

During our year at Hebron, Debindra proved to be a faithful servant to our family. He was such a pleasant little man to have around, such a perfect gentleman. We loved him and began praying for his salvation. How we coveted him for the Lord! Debindra shared much of his early life with us as we often talked together. It was fascinating to learn about the steps that led him into our lives.

He was born in a low-caste Hindu family in Rangamati, the capital town of the Chittagong Hill Tracts. His father, who died when Debindra was five, was considered a learned man. He had distinguished himself as a *kabiraj* (an unlettered country doctor) who knew how to make and prescribe herbal medicines. Debindra was one of five sons of a second marriage.

"We were very strict Hindus," he recalled. "Every Friday was the day of *Loki puja* [worship of Loki]. The women and children especially enjoyed this day. Women placed offerings of bananas, coconuts, sugar or rice before the idol of Loki. At the end of the day all the offerings would be divided up between the children."

As he grew to manhood, he often questioned the meaning of his religion. He married at a very early age and lived on a small farm in the Chittagong Hill Tracts. Finding he needed extra money, he opened a laundry shop in the town of Rangamati. For a while things went smoothly; then his life was disrupted. In 1960, when American engineers completed a hydroelectric dam project on the Karnaphuli River at Kaptai, thousands of families were displaced. The dammed waters backed up for miles into the hills surrounding Rangamati, submerging Debindra's land. He and his family were among those who were displaced.

A refugee now, Debindra was dependent on the government for new land. Thousands like him would have to be relocated somewhere in the country—on land owned or controlled by the government. Helpless to do anything on his own, Debindra's family accepted land many miles to the south—a place that brought them within the width of a river from our home in Hebron.

"Had you ever heard about Christ before you came here?" I asked him.

He thought a minute, then nodded. "Twice before. Once a leper who had been healed came to my laundry. I had heard that many lepers had converted to Christianity, and asked him if this were true. 'Yes,' he said, and added, 'I'm a Christian too.'" Instead of asking the man more about the Christian faith, Debindra scolded him for having changed his religion!

"Then another time when I was doing laundry for a foreign engineer, who worked on the hydroelectric project, a small golden pin fell out of a shirt pocket. I looked to see if it were real gold, and decided it wasn't. I tossed it in the grass, then later got to worrying that maybe it was *tabij* [good luck charm]; so I recovered it and gave it to the engineer. He said it wasn't a good luck charm but a cross, the symbol of Christianity. He didn't say anything more about his beliefs."

Twice then, he had come close to hearing about the Lord, but now, working for us, he was hearing about Him every day!

A year later we had to leave Hebron to reopen the work in the city of Chittagong. Several new missionaries were coming from the States to join us, and this meant helping them find homes and getting them settled in language study.

Debindra hated to see us go. It would mean the loss of a major portion of his monthly income. But even more, he had come to love our family as we did his. He would feel empty and lonely without us. I had an idea. "Why don't you come to Chittagong with us? We'll need a laundryman there too."

Debindra knew that Chittagong was eighty miles away. His wife's relatives lived in one of the suburbs. "Sahib," he replied, his eyes full of tears, "I'd love to go, but if I leave now I might lose my land. The government hasn't given me any papers on it yet. And you know how many boundary disputes there have been between other refugees. I have to get the matter settled."

We moved to Chittagong, leaving Debindra behind. But several months later, a discouraged, lonesome Debindra came to Chittagong in search of us. He had made up his mind to work for us if we would give him a job. We were delighted to see him again, and we hired him to do our washing and also act as night watchman to protect our home. Professional thieves were always busy in the large city, breaking into houses in the dead of night and fleeing with anything they could find.

With his employment secure, Debindra returned to Hebron to get his family. He rented his land to another refugee farmer and then moved to Chittagong to a Hindu village near our new home.

One starry, moonlit night after reporting for work, Debindra and I sat down and talked for several hours about spiritual matters. I shared with him how I came to know Christ as my Savior. "I wasn't born a Christian," I said. (Most Bengalis find this hard to understand. Surely all Americans are Christians. They come from a Christian country!) "I was twelve years old before I first understood the gospel and asked Jesus to forgive my sins and save me." Debindra listened thoughtfully. I told him about my blessed hope and how Christ was going to return someday. Pointing to the cloudless night sky, I said, "Jesus will come in the clouds one day to receive all Christians to Himself." I urged him to make sure he was ready for that event.

Quietly Debindra began to rehearse all the things I had discussed with him during our times at Hebron. As I listened to his soft stammer, I realized that he was finally getting the complicated puzzles of life into a meaningful combination. The strange coincidences that brought us together ... the chance meeting on the path to Lama Bazar ... the warnings from the priests . . . his daughter's death . . . and the decision to follow us to Chittagong. All of this came flowing into Debindra's mind and out in speech. He was finally persuaded to accept Jesus Christ as Savior and Lord!

What a transformation in a man's life! Debindra was exploding with joy. He radiated the love of Christ. The assurance of salvation that filled his heart was something he desperately wanted his beloved wife and children to share.

As God in His providence allowed, it was the death of our beloved missionary friend, Harry Goehring, that Debindra used to finally lead Promilla into the Way Everlasting.

Nine months after Harry died, the Memorial Christian Hospital at Malumghat officially opened. It is located sixty-five miles south of Chittagong. Debindra and his family, along with the missionaries, moved to Malumghat to begin the medical work in 1966. He was hired to be in charge of the hospital laundry, where he serves today.

The most outstanding quality of this tiny man with the stammering tongue is his steadfast love for Christ and his quiet, unobtrusive efforts to win his neighbors. He has won a number of his fellow Bengalis to Christ and influenced many more to consider the claims of the gospel.

One day after moving to Malumghat, he came to me for advice. "Sahib, you know that Hindu village down the road about a half mile south of the hospital? Well, there's a man there who wants to sell his land and move to India. I could buy it and move my family there. We could then be a witness to those around us."

There was only one problem. He would need a loan to do it. But as I pondered the implications of "planting a Christian family" in a heathen village, I decided it would be worth the minimal risk. Debindra purchased the land and built a large mud house—the largest in the village. Together we sank a well to supply the entire village with good water. They would have drinking water, but more important, Debindra would be offering them Living Water for their souls.

In spite of Satan's attacks, Debindra's vision is slowly being fulfilled. Today there are several Christian families who have joined with him. A weekly prayer meeting is providing the groundwork for an indigenous church in a place where none has ever been!

Promilla and Debindra

Debindra and Jay Walsh

5

SHABITRI BARUA
First Christian wedding

IT WAS A BEAUTIFUL morning—her wedding day! Shabitri Barua and Gonijon Tipperah would soon be married. This would be the social event of the year. In fact, theirs would be the first Christian wedding to be celebrated by the newly organized Memorial Baptist Church of Malumghat.

Missionary nurse Becky Davey was acting as mother of the bride. (Missionary nurse Mary Lou Brownell, Shabitri's spiritual mother, was on furlough at this time.) In her special role, Becky found herself extremely busy with all the wedding arrangements.

The bride's own mother had died of a strange fever when Shabitri was a young child. After Shabitri's conversion to

Christ, she began to work for the missionaries doing menial tasks. She was willing to do anything to help support her poor family who lived in a small bamboo hut a short distance from the mission compound. At that time, her jobless father asked the missionary nurses if they would raise his daughter and be responsible for her future.

Becky had purchased a beautiful red silk wedding sari for the radiant bride-to-be. There were golden bangles for her arms, silver hairpieces and a pair of colorful sandals to complete her attire.

Next, of course, was the tremendous job of preparing the wedding feast. This would be one of the most expensive aspects of the marriage celebration. On that festive occasion several hundred guests, friends and relatives of the couple would be attending. Mutton, chicken and fish curries were among the delicacies to be served.

Becky and several of Shabitri's girl friends helped the petite, dark-haired bride into her garments. Her brown skin glowed with a fresh application of coconut oil. Her beautiful white teeth showed in a tremulous smile. "Shabi" (as we nicknamed her) smiled a lot these days!

Then Becky twisted Shabi's waist-long hair into a roll on the back of her head and fastened it with jeweled ornaments. Marks of glowing cosmetics were painted on her forehead following the Bengali tradition. At last the bride was made ready for her handsome bridegroom.

The bridal party was escorted to the church altar where they were united in marriage after saying their vows and exchanging rings and *leis* (flower chains).

The ceremony was over at last, and jubilant guests rang bells and shot off firecrackers while wedding songs blasted forth from a portable megaphone. People in the surrounding villages knew that something exciting was happening. The newlyweds were escorted with great ceremony to the reception hall where they received gifts and then participated in the delicious feast that had been cooked over open fires.

This was a most happy occasion—not just because this special couple was married at last, but because God had ordained that Shabi become a pastor's wife. Her husband was one of the keen young pastors of the Memorial Baptist Church.

Shabi had come a long way from the time when she first came to know us. She would never forget that day. "My sari was tattered and dirty. I had no shoes on my feet. Under my arm I carried a bunch of bananas. These would be my gift to the missionaries. How I hoped that Walsh Sahib would accept them and give me work!"

She was only eleven then and seemed so frail, but we gave her some work so she could help buy food for her family. She carried drinking water from a well about a half mile away. Each day she made several trips to keep us supplied with good drinking water.

But carrying water wasn't easy. The large clay pots when filled weighed over twenty-five pounds. One morning she appeared at our door with swollen, tear-filled eyes. "I can't carry water anymore," she sobbed. "My stepmother has just beaten me with a bamboo rod. My back is bleeding and sore."

We sent the young girl to Mary Lou Brownell, who tenderly treated the large bleeding welts at the mission dispensary. Mary Lou and Shabi soon became good friends. Occasionally Mary Lou would go to Shabi's Buddhist village to tell Bible stories to Shabi and the other village girls.

"As I look back," Shabi recalls, "I wonder if maybe I wasn't a nuisance to her. I would beg her to tell me a Bible story, but the Buddhist priest didn't appreciate her visits to my village. They would threaten me when she would leave. Finally Brownell Missahib had to stop coming, but she didn't give up. She invited us girls to the mission's bamboo schoolhouse to hear the stories. I would sneak away every time I got the chance. It was there I first came to understand."

Mary Lou was a busy nurse, but she was never too busy to help someone come to know the Lord. Sometimes Shabi would arrive in the compound early in the morning and call, "Missahib, Missahib, where are you?" Miss Brownell would lay aside her book or her work and go to greet the young girl. "Are you ill, Shabi?" she would ask, remembering the beatings the girl had received. "No," Shabi would say, "I just want to hear more stories about Jesus. They're such fun!"

Mary Lou often wondered if she was making any spiritual progress with the young Buddhist girl. "The stories I tell you are true, Shabi," she said. "They are not just fun stories. They are about the only true and living God and His Son Jesus Christ."

"Yes, I know," Shabi would say carelessly. But Mary Lou knew she really didn't know—not yet!

Many, many days were spent in teaching, teaching and reteaching the lessons of the Bible. Missionary Mary Lou would use her flannelboard to illustrate spiritual truths. She remembers once putting up three crosses. Two had black hearts (representing sin) attached to the crosspieces. The central cross had a pure white heart.

"Remember when Jesus died on the cross, two thieves were crucified with Him?" Mary Lou reviewed. "One thief said wicked things and cursed Jesus Christ. What happened when he died?"

Shabi was always quick with the right answer. She was a bright child and liked to show her knowledge to the other girls in the class. "He died and went to Hell, bearing his own sins and guilt," the reply came. Then she continued, "The other thief was sorry for his sins and asked Jesus to take him to Heaven with Him."

Mary Lou was pleased that the facts of the stories were getting through, but oh, how she wanted to see evidence that *faith* was taking hold in the girl's life! The lesson would be over. They would sing a song, have a final prayer; then Mary Lou would escort them to their village homes, insuring their safety.

Were her faithful efforts a waste of time? she wondered. Was it worth it all? Shabi knew the right answers, but as yet there was no real salvation. Mary Lou continued to pray for all the girls and for Shabi in particular.

Then one morning as Mary Lou was finishing her breakfast, an excited girl came running to the mission house. "Missahib, oh, Missahib, are you home?" she called. Mary Lou looked into Shabi's dark, tear-sparkled eyes and sensed that the Spirit of God had been dealing with her. "Does God think I have a sinful heart?" Shabi asked in a troubled voice.

"God is waiting to give you a new heart, Shabi," Mary Lou explained. "But you must believe in God's Son, Jesus Christ. You must believe with all your heart—not just your head. This also means forsaking your old religion."

That was the day that Shabi bowed her head and her heart and asked Jesus to save her. The happy girl's eyes were misty with tears. And Mary Lou knew that her prayers had been answered. Her many months of teaching had paid off.

But for Shabi, this was just the beginning. The birth process is so important, but the care and feeding of the newborn infant are vital too. Nurses serving on foreign mission fields are especially aware of this. The high mortality rate of newborn infants in Bangladesh is usually due to lack of proper care—or the wrong kind of care. Just so, helping an individual to experience spiritual growth in Christ is so very necessary in a new believer's life.

The teaching would now continue in earnest. Mary Lou was thrilled daily to see growth in her young friend's life. As yet, Shabi couldn't read or write, but she was quick to grasp many deeper Bible truths because the Holy Spirit was now indwelling her.

Once Shabi told Mary Lou about some of their Buddhist religious customs. "We had a gift tree in the village near the temple," she said. "Worshipers hang money, food and clothing on it. The people believe these gifts are taken up into heaven so when their relatives die, they'll have money, food and clothing up there."

Mary Lou's smile betrayed her unbelief. "Who accepts the gifts, Shabi? Has anyone ever seen them lifted up to heaven?"

Shabi laughed. "Oh, everybody knows the Buddhist priest takes the gifts into the temple as soon as the people leave. But our people really think they'll get them all back when they die. The priests tell them that, and of course, they must believe everything the priest says." Shabi told of one extremely poor family who had no money or gifts to place on the tree. She remembers their tears of sorrow after a loved one died quite suddenly. He would have nothing to use or enjoy in his future life!

Mary Lou used this illustration to teach her young convert spiritual truths. "Did you know that God has a gift tree, Shabi?"

"He does? Where is it?"

"God's gift tree was the cross of Calvary. It was there He placed His greatest gift, His only Son Jesus Christ. He did this so you and everybody else in the world could be saved from sin's penalty."

"If only all my people could understand this," Shabi sighed.

Then Mary Lou impressed upon Shabi the importance of witnessing to others so they could also be saved. "The Bible teaches us that we *can* send something on to Heaven." Opening the Bible she read, "But lay up for yourselves treasures in heaven, where neither moth nor rust doth corrupt, and where thieves do not break through nor steal: for where your treasure is, there will your heart be also" (Matt. 6:20, 21).

When it came time for Mary Lou's furlough in America, Shabi felt her heart would break. The year would go by very quickly for the missionary, who would be with relatives and friends. But for Shabi it would be a long, difficult year in the Buddhist village.

Somehow the year passed, and when Mary Lou returned to Bangladesh, Shabi was elated. Her dearest earthly friend would be near again. But the missionary nurse had sad news. Instead of living at Hebron near Shabi's home, she was going to live in the seaport city of Chittagong, eighty-five miles from the Hebron station!

When they learned the news, the village young people began to taunt Shabi. "She's going to live in the city. What will you do now? You can't stay here and be a Christian much longer. Your father will marry you off to a Buddhist. Then what will you do?"

Those were terrifying days for Shabi. Without the missionary to guide and protect her, she would certainly be forced to marry an unsaved man. She had observed how Christian missionaries treated their wives with love and respect. She couldn't bear to think of spending a lifetime in the darkness of heathendom, especially since she now knew the light of the gospel in her life.

"Take me with you," she begged, tearfully. "Please, please take me with you. I can't stay in the village."

Mary Lou was troubled. She knew in her heart that Shabi was right. Yet there would be so many problems if she took Shabi to the city. How could the girl adjust to the busy city life after living in the village? The problem of feeding her was also a great obstacle. Shabi would want rice and curry and hot chilies all the time. Missionaries often eat the Bengali dishes, but they prefer their own American dishes. Problems! Problems!

She tried to discourage the girl again, but Shabi wasn't to be denied. "Please don't leave me," she sobbed. "I'll eat anything you prepare. Just take me with you." Then she presented a most logical argument. "If I stay here in the village, the leaders will force me to carry food offerings to the temple priest. If I refuse, my stepmother will beat me and deny me food to eat. The village priest will arrange a marriage with someone of the Buddhist faith. It will be *impossible* for me to live here as a lone Christian girl!"

After more thought and prayer and talking it over with her colleague Becky Davey, Mary Lou invited Shabi to live with them in Chittagong.

"What if the answer had been no?" Shabi said later. "Where would I be now? Probably slaving in the muddy rice fields and cooking rice for an unbelieving husband. I would be in captivity and not be able to worship the true God."

But the missionaries had said *yes*. And that involved personal sacrifice. Shabi was to learn in the days to follow that a missionary's life is continually one of sacrifice: giving up homeland, leaving parents and loved ones behind, sacrificing personal desires and ambitions so that others can find new life in Christ. Someday, Shabi determined, she would be like the missionaries!

In Chittagong she learned to read and write. No longer would she be illiterate. Then in 1966 the Memorial Christian Hospital was opened at Malumghat, sixty-five miles south of Chittagong and much nearer Shabi's old village home.

Now it was moving time again, because nurses were needed to work in the hospital. Shabi also moved to Malumghat, for there was work for her to do! Having learned to read and write, Shabi was now qualified to assist in the hospital outpatient department. What a thrilling day it was for her to put on a uniform and begin work! God was going to use her to help others, not only to alleviate their physical sufferings, but to help them come to know the Lord Jesus Christ. She was being a missionary to her own people!

One day a well-educated young man came to work at the hospital. The missionaries were impressed with Gonijon's unusual spiritual insight into the Word of God. He was a capable preacher, and in due time he was called to be the senior pastor of Memorial Baptist Church. Love bloomed at Malumghat, and soon there were whispers about a wedding!

Now the bells were ringing, announcing to everyone that Shabitri Barua and Gonijon Tipperah were married. Shabi, now a pastor's wife, could also hear joy bells ringing in her heart!

6
SYEED UL HOQ
Dare to be a Daniel

SYEED UL HOQ, a new believer, sat cross-legged before me, listening intently as I expounded the Old Testament Book of Daniel. Beside him sat a dozen other men. Some had traveled many miles on foot to attend our annual short-term Bible school at Malumghat, home of the Memorial Christian Hospital.

This year, 1966, my colleague Mel Beals and I were conducting the Bible school. It was a thrill for us to watch these men, most of whom were illiterate, drink in the Word of God. Like a nest full of baby robins stretching to receive their mother's food, these men grasped at every truth we held forth.

It was Syeed, however, who seemed to be completely awed by the Word of God. Between sessions we would find him in a secluded spot reading the Book of Daniel, puzzling over its contents. After the week was over, this rather timid, soft-spoken young man came to me.

"Sahib," he said thoughtfully, "this has been the best week of my life. I want to change my name. From now on, please call me Daniel!"

Little did Syeed realize (or did he?) that his new Christian name would be one he would courageously have to live up to in the years to follow. My fellow missionaries and I would agonize in prayer for him on many occasions as he faced unbelievable persecution.

But Syeed's story doesn't begin here. We must go back to the year that God in His providence allowed a great natural disaster to permanently influence Syeed's life and bring him into contact with Christian missionaries.

In October 1960, during the night hours, a strong wind began to shake Syeed's house on the island of Kutubdia. This island, shaped like a man's footprint, lies barely a mile off the Bangladesh coast just south of the seaport city of Chittagong. As the night wore on, the storm intensified into a killer cyclone and tidal wave that left thousands of helpless people dead or homeless.

For Syeed, his wife and small daughter, that October night was a nightmare they wished they could forget. They lived in a small bamboo hut barely a quarter mile from the beach. That evening, following a hard day's work in the rice paddies, they retired after enjoying a tasty meal of rice and fish curry.

Syeed recalled the events of that night: "We tried to sleep, but the gale force winds frightened us. We huddled together in one corner of the house, waiting for the wind and rain to subside. But they didn't. Shortly we heard the cow shed collapse and two bullocks begin to bellow. I went out to see what had happened, but the wind blew out my lantern and forced me back inside. Still later we felt dampness on our mud floor. Suddenly we were being buoyed up by a forceful surge of water. Horrified, we waded into the yard and climbed a large mango tree which stood beside the house. There we clung to each other and the tree branches until dawn when the storm subsided."

"At dawn, we were still in the tree," Syeed remembers. "A strange thing happened then. A bird flew in from nowhere and started singing a cheerful song. It seemed so incongruous! All around us was death and destruction, but in our tree sat a happy bird. This came as an omen to me. Somehow I felt that God—wherever He was—had been very gracious to us. Perhaps He had spared our lives for something special."

As Syeed surveyed the damage, he realized he had literally been wiped out. His house was wrecked. His cows and poultry were dead. He gathered up what possessions he could find in the mud and silt and moved in with his uncle who lived in the center of the island and had survived the storm. After several weeks of extreme inconvenience (crowded conditions and scarcity of food), Syeed decided to move his family near his wife's relatives on the mainland. This decision brought him to the village of Dhumkali, about a half mile from Malumghat where the Memorial Christian Hospital would one day be built. God had begun that "something special" in Syeed's life.

In 1963 the final selection of land for the site of Memorial Christian Hospital was made at Malumghat, located in the heart of Bangladesh's most beautiful national forest. In the same year construction began on the hospital and missionary houses. Syeed was among the several hundred laborers hired to clear the land and build. In due time our building contractor, Tom McDonald from La Palma, California, found it necessary to hire several guards to watch the property and building materials. He had found that pilfering was all too common! Syeed was one of those guards selected.

For a Christmas present in 1964, Tom and Olline McDonald had bought their Buddhist cook, Monindra, a new Bengali Bible. Monindra treasured it as a gift of love from his sahib and memsahib. Evenings after work he would sit and read in his bamboo hut on the hospital property.

Little did Monindra realize that outside his house, inquisitive, prying eyes were watching him. Syeed, while making his rounds, would stop and peer through the cracks in the bamboo walls. How he wanted to know why Monindra was so intrigued with that book!

One evening he stopped at Monindra's door and began to talk to him. After some small talk, he pointed to the large black book with bright red edges. "Where did you get that book?" he asked.

Monindra, being proud and extremely jealous of his new possession, replied, "That's a Christian Bible. McDonald Sahib gave it to me."

Syeed reached for the book, but before he could touch it, Monindra grabbed it away exclaiming, "Keep your hands off! That's my book!" (His real feeling probably was that he didn't want anyone to defile the Christian Bible.)

Syeed quickly devised a plan. The next day while Monindra was at work, he entered the house and "borrowed" the Holy Book. Then, slipping away to a secluded spot, he read until just before the cook came off duty. Later he replaced the Bible and secured the door so Monindra wouldn't know.

For nearly a week he repeated the process. However, he soon neglected his job as his heart was stirred by the living words. One afternoon another guard informed Tom that Syeed, who had reported for work, was missing. Tom and Olline began to search the compound. From the flat roof of one of the partially constructed houses they heard a moaning sound. When they climbed the ladder, they found Syeed on his knees before the open Bible, crying out in Bengali, "*Probhu Jishu, Probhu Jishu, ahmake rokka koro, ahmake rokka koro!* [Lord Jesus, Lord Jesus, save me, save me!]"

We missionaries would later refer to Syeed's conversion as a true Holy Spirit conversion. This man had come to know and love Jesus as his personal Savior apart from any direct preaching or teaching of a missionary. No doubt the sweet Christian lives of the McDonald family had made their impact.

Sometime after this event, Tom sent me a letter in Chittagong, where we were living after returning from furlough in June 1965. "There's a man here who has a deep interest in the Bible," he wrote. "Would you come down and talk with him? He says he wants a Bible."

On my next trip to visit the McDonalds at Malumghat, I

carried a new Bible. The opportunity to talk with Syeed soon came, and I heard about his conversion firsthand. On that day he had just completed reading Matthew 24, when he called upon the Lord to save him.

"You asked for a Bible," I reminded him. "Do you really want one? Won't it be dangerous if your fellow villagers find out? And besides, a new Bible costs ten rupees [approximately $2]."

"I don't care if it costs one hundred rupees," he said emphatically. "I must get a copy."

The act of obtaining his own Bible was the spark which ignited the persecution that was to come! Fellow Muslims began to heckle him. They called him "Christian" even though he had not yet been baptized. (From the Muslim's viewpoint, believer's baptism indicates the final renunciation of the former religion.) "You are a pork-eater," they would say. (This is the ultimate insult to a Muslim.) They harassed his wife and daughters. Once when his oldest daughter was carrying her father's lunch to him, the men grabbed the container and dumped it on the ground.

In the fall of 1965 we were the first missionaries to take up residence at Malumghat. Once there and settled, I started Bible classes. Syeed attended faithfully.

The hospital was officially opened in March 1966 with a special dedication service. The physical plant and the entire staff was committed to God for His greater glory. Their mission completed, the McDonalds returned to America. The medical/surgical evangelistic work was now to begin in earnest.

During that first year of operation, God blessed His Word in an unusual way. Attendance at the weekly Bible classes grew. A number of people professed faith in Christ, necessitating a baptismal service. It would be the first one ever to be witnessed in that area. It was a beautiful sunny day. The location was a small, isolated pond in a nearby forest. Perhaps one hundred people, most of them coming out of curiosity, looked on. On that memorable occasion eleven believers, including Syeed, were baptized as friends—and enemies—watched!

Syeed, now Daniel, dared to take his stand! Immediately after the baptismal service, rumors spread that an angry group of Muslims were going to lynch Daniel! We could only commit him to the Lord in prayer.

The following day Daniel failed to report for work. The labor-foreman reported that he was sick. I was told the same story the following day. Feeling uneasy about the matter, I called a trusted Muslim friend and asked him about Daniel. This man, secretly interested in the gospel himself, confided that Daniel had been severely beaten, exiled to the island of Kutubdia, and placed in the care of relatives. His wife and children were left in Dhumkali to care for their property.

I was frustrated and angry. But there was nothing I could do but pray and commit Daniel to the Lord's keeping. I shared the news with my fellow missionaries and national believers. Daniel became the special object of intercessory prayer. During the weeks to follow, we heard very little news of Daniel. One rumor, however, was very distressing. Daniel was reported to have been blinded as a result of his severe beating!

Three months after Daniel's exile, I was walking on the road near the hospital when a man approached me. His head had been shaved bald. I could hardly believe my eyes! It was Daniel, and he wasn't blind! He embraced me warmly according to the Muslim custom. (When special friends meet, they embrace, touching chests three times.) I kept him busy answering a barrage of questions. "What happened? Where have you been? How did you get here? Are you still in danger?"

Daniel rehearsed how he had contrived an escape from Kutubdia in a Hindu-owned fishing sampan. He shaved off his hair to change his appearance. Reaching the mainland, he had hurried to find me. Since he was still in great danger, I made provision for him to live within the hospital compound. But news of Daniel's return was soon being whispered around every village fire. The "bamboo telegraph" is very efficient in Bangladesh!

Shortly after his return, he sat in our short-term Bible school and learned about Daniel the prophet, a series I had been teaching. It was also at this time that Dr. Robert T. Ketcham, father of Dr. Donn Ketcham our fellow missionary, came to visit his son. I invited the beloved preacher to bring several messages on Psalm 23. (These famous messages in book form, *I Shall Not Want*, have blessed thousands of people in America.) During the final message, Daniel was mysteriously called out of the meeting. "Your relatives want to see you," he was told.

Leaving us, he went outside to find about one hundred

*Bible school with missionary Mel Beals;
"Daniel" in center*

village men waiting for him, insisting that he go with them. "No," Daniel said firmly, holding up his Bible for them to see; "I am a Christian now."

The crowd became noisy, but missionaries were able to disperse them and Daniel returned to the meeting, shaken and frightened. As he went back into the service, he arrived just in time to hear the final words of Dr. Bob's message: "I will fear no evil, for Thou art with me." This timely exhortation was just what Daniel needed!

Once again, he became the target of persecution. Like angry jackals after their prey, fanatical Muslims, encouraged by village priests, made every effort to arrest him again. Daniel was secure within the confines of the hospital compound, so persecution took another form. Villagers began to harass his wife and small children who lived only a half mile away. First they refused to let her bathe in the public pond. Then they forbade her or the children to pump water from the village well. Each time she sent reports to me of harassment, I would go to the village leader on her behalf. This intervention would prove successful only for a few days.

Then, in the middle of the night, Daniel's frightened wife came to us, bringing her children. Shaken and breathless, she reported threats of being burned alive inside her house. In the dark hours of the night, male voices had threatened, "We are going to pour gasoline around your house and set it afire if you don't divorce your husband!"

Life had become so unbearable for her that we were able to convince Daniel's wife that she should join her husband on the hospital compound. This she did reluctantly, fearing more reprisals from her relatives. She was still a Muslim and had mixed feelings about her husband's new faith.

Even with the whole family living as refugees on the compound, persecution still persisted. Late one night the hospital guard fired a shotgun blast into the air above their house to disperse a gang of villains who were trying to kidnap Daniel's wife. Before the alarm was sounded, however, the hoodlums had managed to rip off part of her clothing. We found her torn sari the next morning in the woods behind their house.

The persecutors, unable to get at Daniel on the hospital compound, tried yet another tactic. A newspaper reporter, whose home was in the area, printed an article in one of the country's leading papers, attacking the hospital and the "nefarious" activities of the Christian missionaries. Among other false information printed was the statement that we had paid Daniel a large sum of money to become a Christian!

The newspaper article brought about an investigation by the police. But our Heavenly Father gave us the victory, and we were able to turn the incident to our favor. The article was so packed with lies and misinformation that investigating authorities dropped the case.

We considered it wise, however, to send Daniel away for several months. We concurred with the suggestion of a police officer that this would relax tension in the area and allow the fanatical fires to subside. Arrangements were made for Daniel and his oldest daughter (who had also professed to be a Christian) to spend a few months with a Christian family in the extreme northern part of Bangladesh.

By the time Daniel returned to Malumghat, the anti-Christian situation had quieted down. His family had once again established themselves in their village home. Daniel, who continued to live on hospital property, made periodic visits to see them without incident.

Life for Daniel was still a struggle. His property, his family, his life, his beliefs were all at stake. Yet his faith in the Lord was unswerving. With the help of his Christian friends, he continued his active role in the developing Christian community.

Daniel was to experience yet one more severe test of his faith. By 1970 the church at Malumghat had made sizable gains. The unstable political situation in the country, coupled with our steady advances for Christ, provided Satan with an excellent opportunity to strike again!

Political opportunists decided to use the hospital as their prime target for gaining public support. Two more slanderous newspaper articles were printed, focusing on missionary activity in general and our medical work in particular. About this time Daniel, who had already begun to move about the countryside with a bit more freedom, ventured into the crowded bazaar only a mile down the road from the hospital. He needed a haircut.

Already angered by the recent newspaper articles, several men recognized him as the Muslim-turned-Christian, and accosted him as he was about to leave the barber shop. They ripped off his shoulder bag, dumping its contents on the ground. They spotted some Christian tracts! "He's not only an infidel, he's preaching the Christian religion. Kill him! Kill him!" they screamed.

Daniel was beaten with umbrellas and sticks and kicked until blood oozed from his body. Young boys were called upon to urinate in his face as he lay half-conscious in the ditch beside the road. But God was aware that His special child was in need of divine intervention. Our hospital ambulance driver "just happened" to come upon the scene as he was returning from a call. Seeing the angry crowd in the road and Daniel in trouble, he sped back to inform Dr. Olsen, who was on duty at the hospital.

Dr. Olsen deserted his patients and raced to the scene in time to save Daniel, who was about to have his tongue cut out! The vicious man with the knife backed away as the crowd dispersed. Daniel was carefully lifted into the ambulance and taken to the hospital where we nursed him back to health.

In all this, Daniel refused to deny his Lord. In 1972, just after the Bangladesh war, he was one of fifty-five believers to become charter members of the Memorial Baptist Church of Malumghat. Subsequently we were able to help Daniel and his family get established on a pineapple plantation—a mission farming project that Mel Beals and I started. Daniel lives there today. He has endured persecution and hardship, proving to his fellow countrymen that his conversion was a genuine experience.

As I reflect upon his Christian life, the words of the apostle Paul to the Corinthians seem amazingly fitting for Daniel: "Thrice was I beaten with rods, once was I stoned ... a night and a day I have been in the deep; in journeyings often, in perils of waters, in perils of robbers, in perils by mine own countrymen ... in weariness and painfulness, in watchings often, in hunger and thirst ... in cold and nakedness" (2 Cor. 11:25-27).

The hymn writer said, "Dare to be a Daniel, Dare to stand alone! Dare to have a purpose firm! Dare to make it known!" These words apply perfectly to Daniel of Bangladesh. His stand for Christ was subsequently to bear fruit.

In February 1974 the following letter was received at Malumghat:

Honorable Dr. Olsen,

> I would like to have the opportunity of inviting your kind attention to the following that the people of this island are very much grateful to your 'Baptist Mission' for their gallant service in humanitarian affairs. Thousands of patients, ill-clad and ill-fed have got proper treatment in your missionary hospital and got recovery. It is you, the 'Baptist Mission' from whom the helpless and the poor and neglected people can expect this sort of humanitarian service.
>
> We, about 65 thousand islanders, will be highly benefited if you kindly extend your honorable humanitarian service here in the shape of establishing a missionary hospital in the Dhurung Union. We will extend our heartiest cooperation in preaching the religion of Christ and will share with you in humanitarian service.
>
> Your earliest response in this regard will be high appreciated. Thanking you.
>
> Faithfully yours,
> M.R.
> B.A. (honors), M.A., B.Ed.

After he had shared the letter with me, I suggested to Dr. Olsen that we visit Kutubdia. He readily agreed. Arrangements were made for the two of us to spend a night there. And who made the arrangements? Who acted as our guide for the entire trip? Syeed ul Hoq—our Daniel! Unbelievable! Daniel, the "infidel and traitor," the persecuted one. Daniel, the Christian, proudly introduced us to his relatives and island leaders!

Dr. Olsen and I had an unforgettable time talking with and witnessing to the people of Kutubdia. They pled with us to return and start a medical work. They welcomed the preaching of the Word! Perhaps the greatest treat of all for us was to learn of eight secret believers on the island, several of whom were Daniel's relatives! We stayed overnight in the home of the one who sent the letter of invitation. He was one of the relatives who took charge of Daniel after he was beaten the first time and sent in exile.

Daniel has suffered much for his faith, but the Heavenly Father has rewarded and honored his steadfastness. Because of his valiant stand, others are coming to know Daniel's God!

7

SHUKIE BAHADUR
Call me Happy

WHAT HAD EVER POSSESSED his mother to call him Shukie? Shukie Bahadur was born in the foothills of the mighty Himalayas in the tiny kingdom of Nepal. Since birth his life had been nothing but one hardship after another.

Life at best is a struggle for millions of poor people living on the Indian subcontinent. Shukie could never remember being truly happy. Yet, at some time, a poor Hindu woman had given birth to a little black-haired boy and called him Shukie. Perhaps she was happy over his arrival. At least the child was a boy instead of a girl. This alone would give the parents some hope for the future. Or, maybe she hoped he would have a happier life than she and her husband had experienced. Anyway, she named him Shukie, which means "happy" in the Bengali language.

Shukie grew to boyhood serving the family idols. As devout Hindus, his family worshiped a pantheon of gods and goddesses of which they believed there were at least 300,000. The daily ritual of offering food or flowers to one of their many gods was something that Shukie had to learn. Trips to the village temple and other holy places were as common to him as eating his daily meals. Reared on fear and superstition, it's no wonder that Shukie was constantly afraid of displeasing the gods!

There was no assurance of the future either. The most he could hope for was a better reincarnation. Since Hindus believe life itself consists of a series of rebirths, they hope to please the deities enough to find a better existence in the next life. It would be horrible to come back as a dog or some kind of bug! So it was that Shukie grew up with fear and uncertainty about the future.

When he was old enough to work, he was hired as a servant boy in the home of a well-to-do family. This meant obeying the numerous commands of his master. He had been born as a low-caste Hindu, so doing menial household chores posed no problem for him. He cleaned the house, prepared food, ran errands, shopped at the bazaar, and watched his master's children. As a remuneration for his round-the-clock labors, he earned his food and a few rupees as wages. This money was turned over to his father to help buy food for the family.

When he was twelve, Shukie's parents moved to Shillong, India, to find work in the tea gardens. Some of the world's best tea is grown in that area of the Indian subcontinent. This poor family moved with the hope that they might better their financial condition by working for British tea owners. (At that time the British were ruling India.) It was in Shillong that Shukie and his family learned the art of picking the choicest tea leaves to be shipped from Calcutta to the markets of the world.

"In Shillong," Shukie remembered, "our family started to

prosper. There was enough money to send me to the government school so I was able to learn to read and write Bengali."

Just as they were beginning to make a decent living, tragedy struck their home. An epidemic of smallpox swept through the area, taking the lives of Shukie's parents. He was alone in the world now, except for an older sister and a younger brother. It seemed best for the three children to separate in order to find employment to maintain themselves. Life had dealt them a cruel blow, but survival was necessary. So Shukie parted from his sister and brother, never to see them again.

For the next thirteen years, Shukie wandered around India. He would work his way from place to place by doing menial jobs. His travels took him to some of India's major cities, including Delhi, Bombay, and the teeming city of Calcutta. He arrived in Calcutta during the height of World War II. The city was humming with activity as Allied troops, destined for combat in southeast Asia, passed through.

In Calcutta Shukie found a job in the home of a British army major, his very first personal contact with someone known as "Christian." (All foreigners were looked upon as Christians by the Indians.) Shukie was inwardly delighted to have this unusual opportunity of serving a foreign sahib!

For six years he worked as the major's personal servant. Cleaning the house, polishing shoes, and generally obeying his every command, such as bringing tea or lighting a cigarette, were among the daily duties of the servant.

"The major was good to me," Shukie recalls. "I had enough food to eat and clothes to wear. That was one of the happiest periods of my life."

But still there was a missing dimension. Day after day he searched for peace of mind. The vacuum in his heart could not be filled. He was curious about the Christian religion. He observed that his master was a devout churchgoer. Each Sunday he would lay out the major's special clothing which he wore to the Anglican church. Shukie was puzzled that the major never took food or flowers to his temple. What kind of god was it that did not require food or flowers as an offering?

But not once did the major offer to share his knowledge of the truth. Many, many years later, as Shukie remembered this time, he realized there was a difference between "professing" and "possessing" Christians. It may well have been that the major was one of the former.

After India gained independence from Great Britain in 1947, Shukie migrated to Chittagong, Bangladesh (then East Pakistan). There he found lodging with a family who befriended him. "I made them my relatives," he said with a grin. "Even to this day they are the only people I have."

Eventually Shukie's "relatives" arranged his marriage to a Hindu girl. And again, there was unhappiness, for the couple was childless. "Probably it was a good thing we had no children," Shukie said. "It was hard enough to feed the two of us on my meager salary of one hundred *takas* per month [$20]. What would we have done with a family?"

Then it happened! Shukie lost *that* job! As he put it, "Luck was against me." The Bengali engineer family he was working for in Chittagong moved away, leaving him jobless. Employment during those days was difficult to find. More sadness!

"For a while we lived off our relatives and friends," Shukie said. "In the meantime, I took to the streets, going from house to house looking for work."

His pursuit of a job in October 1960 brought him to our door. We had just moved to Chittagong from Hebron a few days before. Someone told him about us. After we examined his letters of reference, we decided to try him as a cook-bearer.

Shukie worked for us until December 1963 when we returned to America on furlough. During those years he heard the gospel message clearly for the first time in his life. He watched us as we had family devotions. He even attended the Bengali church services on occasion. But his superstitious heart and mind refused to bow to the Lord Jesus Christ.

After our departure, Shukie found another job, this time with an English businessman in Chittagong. Reflecting on that year he said, "Whatever bad luck I'd had before, it grew worse after you left. For 1964 was the year my fortune went bad. [This expression is used to indicate extreme bad luck.] My wife died and left me all alone in the world. Then, there was that accident. . . ."

One day he attended a championship soccer match in the Chittagong stadium. When the game was over, while leaving with the crowds, he accidently stepped into a sewer hole, wrenching his hip out of joint. For more than a year he was out of work while his hip healed enough for him to get around.

"I sold my watch and most of my household goods in order to have food," he said.

He recovered well enough to look for work, and this time he came in contact with our fellow missionary Reid Minich. This began a warm relationship between the two men, one that Reid capitalized upon to share his faith. Shukie politely listened to his employer but still was not ready to forsake his Hindu beliefs.

Then another unhappy accident occurred. While stepping off a city bus (buses never come to a full stop!) Shukie lost his balance and fell on the other leg, severely damaging the knee. Treatments in the local hospital didn't seem to help much. He continued to walk with a limp and shuffling gait, making it difficult for him to continue his work. Days later Reid observed that Shukie's hip problem was also getting increasingly worse. He had a deeper, swaying limp now and complained of extreme pain.

"We ought to do something for Shukie," Reid said to me one day. "He is finding it more and more difficult to work."

Reid and I discussed the possibility of admitting Shukie to the Memorial Christian Hospital for hip surgery. We knew, however, that he had no financial resources to cover such an operation. So we determined to bear the cost.

The Memorial Christian Hospital, sixty-five miles south of Chittagong, had been the means of many hundreds of people receiving physical and spiritual healing. The most capable doctors and nurses in the country worked there. They not only treated the sick, but the gospel message was also freely dispensed. Their reasoning was: What profit is there in saving the body if the soul goes to an eternal Hell? Medical/surgical EVANGELISM was their goal!

It was time for Reid's furlough, but before he left, he called Shukie. "If you are willing to undergo surgery, Mr. Walsh and I will pay for it. It's up to you." Fellow missionaries Willard and Donna Benedict promised to do their part and see that Shukie was properly cared for and fed during his hospitalization. (Relatives or friends are expected to prepare food and care for the needs of the patient while he is in the hospital.)

Shukie was certainly grateful for the offer. He realized now that his missionary friends really loved him and wanted to help. Yet, he was not sure he could face such an ordeal. It would certainly mean a lot more pain and discomfort. All his life he had experienced pain of one kind or another. Could he go through any more? As he continued to mull over the offer in his mind, he reasoned: "If the operation is successful, I might be able to walk without that bamboo cane. It is such a nuisance!"

The doctors were his friends, he told himself. He knew Dr. Ketcham and Dr. Olsen from their many visits to the homes in which he had worked. He could trust them. He also knew that Reid Minich and the Walsh family loved him and were concerned for his well-being. Certainly he would not be among strangers if he went to the hospital at Malumghat.

Shukie was admitted to Memorial Christian Hospital on November 25, 1967. Dr. Donn Ketcham and Dr. Vic Olsen prepared him for surgery.

On the day before surgery, while making his rounds, Dr. Olsen picked up the Bible from the table beside Shukie's bed. "Shukie, friend, you need to be born again. Did you know that?" Dr. Olsen said. "One birth is not enough." This concept certainly must have appealed to Shukie's Hindu-oriented mind! Then Vic took time from his busy schedule to explain the story of Nicodemus before leaving the room.

A short time later one of the Bengali Christians visited Shukie. As they talked, this person also witnessed to him about the necessity of the new birth.

Still later in the day, I stopped to visit with Shukie and give him a few encouraging words. "Cheer up, friend, tomorrow at this time the operation will be over, and you'll have a new hip!"

Shukie was anything but happy. In fact, he looked very unhappy. I felt a strong impulse to talk very seriously with him about his lost condition. Not realizing that two others had already witnessed to him about the new birth, I, too, picked up the Bible and opened to John chapter three. He received three preoperative injections of that chapter in a matter of hours!

"I'll receive Christ sometime," he told me as I put the question to him. "Maybe before I leave the hospital."

One thing was certain. Shukie would have to convalesce for several months after the operation. The doctors would have to open the hip and implant a new stainless steel hip joint.

"Sometime may be too late," I said. "Suppose something happens to you, Shukie. Suppose you never have another chance to accept Christ after today."

He turned his face away and stared out the window. "After the operation, then I'll decide," he said rather adamantly.

"But the Bible says there is danger in putting off such a big decision. In fact, God says, 'Today is the day of salvation.' Shukie, you can ask God to save you right now, and He will."

He reflected for a few moments, then looking squarely into my face, he surprised me. "Yes. I'm ready *right now* to become a Christian. I've made up my mind!"

How gratifying to help this poor Hindu call upon the life-giving name of Jesus for the forgiveness of sins. Later he confessed that his hip problem was worth it all. Because of it, he found the Savior!

The operation the next day went as scheduled. The doctors fitted his new hip joint in place and sewed up the incision. Soon Shukie was convalescing in one corner of the male ward. Days stretched into weeks, weeks into months. We waited and prayed that the hip would heal properly.

During this period we came to know Shukie well. The radiance of his face seemed to warm us before we reached his bedside. He loved the new Bible given him by a friend. When we would come, he would be so engrossed in the Scriptures that he was hardly aware of visitors. He was literally feasting constantly on the Word of God!

One afternoon I asked, "Shukie, what have you been reading today?"

He turned with face aglow and said, "I'm reading all over, here and there. Just all over. It's *all* so interesting! So far I've read through Genesis and Exodus in the Old Testament. Then I skipped to the New Testament and have read Matthew and John. I've read all of Hebrews and Revelation. You know, Sahib, I love Revelation best of all!"

Spending months in a hospital bed is not too pleasant for anyone. So one day I scooped up an armful of old *National Geographic* magazines, thinking Shukie might enjoy looking at the pictures. It would break the monotony for him.

The next visit I noted that the stack of magazines had not been touched. "You know, Sahib," he explained, "I've still got a lot of things to learn about the Bible. I really haven't had the time to look at those other books you gave me!"

Shukie's stay in the hospital stretched from a few months to two years! One night in his sleep he wrenched the new hip joint apart. This required a second operation by Dr. Ketcham. However even with the best surgical care available, Shukie would never walk again without the aid of crutches or a wheelchair. In spite of all the good medicines and medical care, his muscles refused to heal properly around the hip joint.

With the same tenacity that spurred him on as a non-Christian, Shukie, with the Lord's help, has accepted his disability and turned it into an asset for the glory of the Savior. Discharged from the hospital, he was engaged as a hospital evangelist. A new wheelchair was imported for his use. A cement sidewalk, dubbed "Shukie's Highway," was poured from his house on the compound to the hospital entrance to facilitate his daily travel. Today he moves freely about the ward and outpatient department, witnessing and telling of Jesus' love to other patients.

"Are you any happier than when you came here two years ago?" I asked him one day.

His thin face lit up with a heavenly smile. "Happy? I never knew what happiness was until I met the Lord. Before I came to the hospital, 'Shukie' was just another name. But now I have found my Savior and discovered the genuine meaning of it. Sahib, please call me *'happy'* from now on!"

8
INDRA BOSHONE
Growing pineapples for the Lord

I SAT AT MY DESK and wearily reached for the next envelope. One by one, all day, people had been coming to me, pressing urgent petitions into my hand.

A lean, thin man with a pockmarked face stood before me. Outside were many others. Hopeless, unhappy people with dark, pleading eyes. Each one hoped that the Christian missionaries would give them help.

We had met so many of these poor, despondent people in 1971. During those terrible months of civil war in Bangladesh, a marauding enemy army stalked the land, burning houses and killing unarmed and innocent Bengalis. Their sad, drawn faces were before me now. Faces of people whose houses had been burned. Men whose wives and daughters had been raped. People whose only hope of finding sympathy and help (they thought) was in the hands of the missionaries.

One after another I read their petitions. Most of them were alike. At least they contained the same message:

> The Chairman
> Memorial Christian Hospital
> Malumghat   12 June 1971
>
> Respected Sir:
>
> I beg to inform you that I am a poor man of Harbang Union, under Police Station Chakaria, District Chittagong. During the recent disturbance, my humble hut and all my earthly possessions were destroyed by fire and all my cattle heads were taken away by the miscreants. Now I am hopeless and cannot provide for my family. Therefore, I kindly request your honorable self to consider my case and supply me with money to rebuild my home. I remain,
>
> Your most obedient servant,
> M.H.

One by one I had listened to their woeful stories and then dismissed them with the promise that we would try to help as funds became available. Now the man with the pockmarked face was before me, bowing in a self-effacing manner. I glanced at the name on the petition he shyly pushed into my hand. "Indra Boshone of Dulahazara." He was a Hindu who lived barely a mile from the hospital. I glanced over his petition and found it to be much like the others with one difference. One line read: "I'm interested to learn more about the Christian religion."

Aha! I thought. He is a clever man. He thinks by inserting that little phrase he will get quick sympathy and early action on his petition! Generally a man who would write such a statement is a self-seeker, and we missionaries had many experiences with such people. So I carefully began to question him. "Where do you live?"

"In the Hindu doctor's village across from the Dulahazara bazaar," he replied.

Villages are often identified by a prominent citizen. I knew where he meant. His village had gained fame because of an educated Hindu doctor who lived there.

"But Sahib," he continued, "I'm only living there temporarily. My own home has been burned to the ground."

Indra Boshone, like thousands of others, had fallen victim to the *goondas* (thugs) who were collaborating with the Pakistan army. All Hindus were considered supporters of the Bangladesh freedom movement. Therefore most of them were victimized in some way or another. Indra had lost everything.

"Your petition says you want to learn more about the Christian religion. Why did you say that?" I asked.

His eyes fell, and he gave a fearful glance around to see if anyone was listening. "Sahib," he said, "I don't have any peace in my heart. People of my religion aren't interested in helping me. And the Muslims want to drive us out of the village. I really meant what I said about wanting to know more about the Christian faith."

Although Indra knew very little about Christianity, he had observed the Christians at Memorial Christian Hospital where he often came selling dried fish to the patients and their families. He had been impressed by the joy exhibited by Christians at the hospital. But more, he had been attracted to Christ by Debindra, the hospital laundryman. (See chapter 4.) Debindra had given temporary shelter to Indra's family after their house was burned. Then when it became necessary for Hindus to hide in the jungles from the army, Debindra went and ministered to them.

"Several families fled to a jungle refuge three miles east of the hospital," Indra told me. "Debindra's family came with us instead of going to Hebron station with the other Bengali Christians who evacuated. Most of us were upset and crying, but Debindra kept telling us about Jesus Christ. He wasn't afraid like the rest of us."

Indra and Debindra were together in hiding for two weeks before returning to Malumghat. When news reached them that the army had left, they returned.

Debindra's Christian witness was to mean even more to Indra soon after this. "A local Muslim leader called all the Hindus together and insisted they all convert to Islam. He gave us a choice: convert or leave the country. We were to go to the mosque and give our *salam* [Muslim greeting meaning "peace"]. Next we were to grab our earlobes and show the priest our humility, then bow in the direction of Mecca and pray. Lastly, we were told we had to be circumcised."

The Hindus, feeling the pressure was being put on them, didn't know what to do. Then Debindra showed up. When the arrogant Muslim leader recognized the Christian laundryman, he fled with his cohorts. The meeting broke up without any of the Hindus having to go to the mosque! Debindra had saved them! Indra told me that Debindra decided to investigate this illegal meeting. He found out that the Muslim leader had made plans to forcefully marry Indra's oldest daughter!

While Indra was in Debindra's care, the little Christian laundryman witnessed to him about Jesus Christ. The young, marriageable daughter was led to the Lord, and Debindra arranged for her to marry a Christian man.

No wonder Indra felt indebted to Debindra! I was convinced that he must, indeed, be interested in learning more about the Christian faith. To test his sincerity, I invited him to attend the Sunday morning church services. The next Sunday he slipped in the back and sat through the service. But he disappeared before I had an opportunity to speak with him.

Each Sunday he would come in, sit in the back, and then quickly leave as soon as the service ended. After several months he came to my office, bringing a stalk of ripe bananas. His smiling face—quite a contrast from the dark, dour look when we had first met—told me something had happened!

"I notice you've been coming to church regularly," I said.

"Yes, and I am now a Christian!" he said, smiling.

"When did it happen?" I asked eagerly.

"Do you remember, Sahib, when an Indian plane dropped the bombs near the hospital just as the war was ending?"

I did indeed! From March until December of 1971 we had witnessed the turmoil of civil war as the Bengali people fought for independence from Pakistan. In early December the Indian armed forces joined the Bengali freedom fighters to topple the Pakistan military regime. At that time an Indian bomber circled near our hospital, dropping two bombs on a building they thought was still under Pakistani military control. The building, the village community center, was less than a half mile from the hospital and only a few hundred yards from Debindra's house where Indra Boshone's family was staying!

"That very night," Indra now said, "I dreamed that I went to the pond to take a bath. I had waded out into deep water, in my dream, and took a plunge. Suddenly it felt like my feet were weighted down, and I couldn't come up for air. As I struggled, in my dream, I heard a voice saying, 'Indra, are you going to continue in the path of darkness, or will you enter the path of light?' But I said, 'I'm a sinner and want to go on in darkness.' A second time I felt myself drowning, and the voice came again, asking me, 'Indra, will you continue on in darkness, or will you come to the light?'"

All of Debindra's faithful witness to Indra was invading his subconscious life. This time, Indra said, in his dream, "I want to enter the light." And the voice said, "Believe in Jesus Christ." Believing the voice to be Jesus Himself, when Indra awoke, he prayed and asked Jesus Christ to save him.

In the morning, Indra told his wife about the dream and how he had asked Christ to save him. Then he shared his testimony with missionary Mel Beals. Now he was rehearsing it with me.

There could be no doubt of his sincerity. He faithfully attended the Sunday services and joined the baptismal class. One month later he announced to his world that he was a Christian by being obedient to the Lord in believer's baptism.

Indra's new faith solved his spiritual problem. His search for peace was over. But he still had no house to call his own. The temporary quarters in the Hindu doctor's village were not satisfactory. People there were beginning to spurn him for becoming a Christian. "Please help me," he said one day. "I want to find a place to live in peace."

His request came just when we had negotiated the purchase of ten acres of hilly jungle land near the hospital. Mel Beals and I planned to start a pineapple and banana plantation which would serve a double purpose: teach our national brethren how to farm hilly land in a scientific manner, and help establish our Christian families on a farm which could support them. This way they would not be dependent on the mission for employment.

The idea of a farming self-help project started with Mel. One day I heard him say, "The missing link between new converts and an indigenous church is financial independence. We need to help the poor Christian to help himself. When Christians are able to maintain a decent living, they will be able to support the church; but not until!"

Mel and I talked with Indra about the project, suggesting that he be one of the first to get involved. He and his family decided to try our plan. Our basic concept was to help his family learn how to make a living off one acre of land! We would select the acre of land, build them a mud house, and plant the plot full of pineapples, bananas and other long-range fruit-bearing trees. Of course, this was only a loan to them. Over a period of several years, after they refunded our investment, the entire project would be theirs to keep.

Indra and his family worked hard cutting the jungle and digging out the stumps. After several weeks, by cooperative effort, a mud house was built for them.

The next step was to teach Indra how to farm the land in a contour fashion so that every foot of his small plot could be cultivated. Then five thousand pineapple shoots were planted, completely filling the acre plot. Interspersed at fifteen-foot intervals were bananas and other fruits.

During the weeks of transforming a jungle hillock into a beautifully clean fruit plantation, Indra had many doubts and misgivings. Would it be successful? Such farming was so new to him! What was that peculiar stuff called *fertilizer* that the missionaries insisted he use? Would it be as good as cow manure? (Bengalis are traditionalists. What was good enough for their forefathers is good enough for them.)

We prodded and encouraged Indra and his family to work faithfully, nurturing the young plants to fruition. Twenty months later the first crop was starting to "head out."

Finally an excited Indra called me to come see his farm! We walked over the acre of land, counting 3,190 pineapples bearing fruit for the first time. Each one would sell for at least thirty cents at harvesttime! What a reward for his labors!

While we taught Indra how to farm and help himself, we also taught him the Christian principles of giving God the firstfruits of his land. Learning to give to the local church has been an exciting part of Indra's Christian experience. He is slowly understanding the principle that it is impossible to outgive the Lord.

Indra, his wife and four daughters are still living on that one acre of former jungle land. The future looks bright for them as together they work, not only to help themselves, but to strengthen the work of the Lord in the local church!

Indra Boshone and banana plant

9

ROBINDRA BARUA
Saved twice

THE HOSPITAL GUARD rapped sharply on our door. "What is it?" I called.

"There's a man from Lama who wants to speak with you." The guard sounded disturbed. "I think maybe you should talk with him. He's crying."

What now, I wondered. Interruptions like this were common, especially during the year of revolution and war in Bangladesh. Daily someone would come to me with a problem: a missing loved one, no food, a death in the family, need of medical assistance, land problems, and so on.

"All right," I told the guard who intercepts all visitors coming to see me. "Bring him here."

Moments later the guard escorted the visitor to the veranda of our house. I recognized the man immediately as Shamakishor Barua from the Bilchari Buddhist village near the mission station at Hebron. In 1960 when we first arrived on the field, he was one of the carpenters hired to help me build a house at Hebron.

"What brings you here, Shamakishor?" I asked, after dismissing the guard. I could see he was deeply troubled.

Overcome with emotion, he just stared into my face for a minute. Then tears rolled from his sad eyes. Several moments passed before he could speak coherently. Then slowly he said, "Sahib, I fear that my son Robindra has been killed. He was taken prisoner by the Pakistani military to their camp at Cox's Bazar. But he may still be alive. Please help us, Sahib. I know my son isn't guilty!"

The year 1971 was one of turmoil and war in Bangladesh (formerly East Pakistan). In March the Bengali people had revolted. For too long the non-Bengali masters had ruled the illiterate masses of the Bengali people in East Pakistan. Now, under the strong leadership of Bengali patriot Sheikh Mujibur Rahman, the nation was in revolt and warfare.

The unarmed Bengalis, however, couldn't contend with the modern weapons of the Pakistan army. By the end of April 1971, the army had fanned out across the country, completely suppressing the rebellion. Ten million fearful Bengalis fled the advancing army and took refuge in India and Burma.

After they had suppressed the rebellion, the army set up military camps throughout the countryside. Then in a systematic pattern they moved from village to village and house to house, searching for hidden Bengali rebels. Their special target became the Hindus and minority groups, whom they accused of collaborating with India in a massive conspiracy to break up Pakistan. Since 1947 when the nation was born, East and West Pakistan had existed in two wings, separated by a thousand miles with India between. East Pakistan, on the Bay of Bengal, was almost completely surrounded by Indian territory. It would be easy for the army to think that the Bengali Hindus and Buddhists were collaborating with India.

It was in just such a search that Robindra, Shamakishor's son, was arrested and accused of supporting the Bengali rebel cause. He, along with a group of other young Bengali boys from Lama Bazar, was taken to the subdivisional town of Cox's Bazar for interrogation.

"When was he arrested?" I asked Robindra's father.

"Two weeks ago," came the reply. "He and some other village boys were talking in a tea stall in the bazaar. Completely surprised, they were tied up and marched away by four military men." Shamakishor's shoulders were stooped. His hands came up to cover his face in despair. Then he begged, "Sahib, isn't there anything you can do to save my son?"

"Why didn't you come to me two weeks ago?" I asked. "Perhaps I could have done something then. It's probably too late now!" From reports and rumors that had been received, there seemed to be no rhyme or reason to the execution process. Some of the so-called rebels were interrogated and tortured; some were summarily shot; still others were kept under arrest for months.

"I didn't think about coming to you right away," the boy's father replied. "It was only yesterday that someone in the village suggested I see Walsh Sahib. So I've come. You are my only hope."

My heart went out to the grieving father who stood before me. While his case seemed hopeless, I still felt the urgency of trying to save the boy if he were still alive. With men I reminded myself, things may be impossible. But with God. . . .

"All right," I told Shamakishor. "Tomorrow morning I'll go to Cox's Bazar and seek information about your son's whereabouts. I don't think there's much hope; but let me try. I'm going to pray and ask the other Christians to pray for God's special guidance in this matter."

Shamakishor thanked me profusely and then left. His shoulders and back straightened as if he were confident that I could fix everything.

But I was not so confident. The rest of the day I was deeply troubled and kept going over in my mind about the wisdom of interfering in this matter. Was I wise in agreeing to speak out in behalf of a young man who had been accused of anti-state activity? Would my interference put me and our entire mission in jeopardy? The Pakistan government might accuse me of supporting the revolt, and we might even be expelled from the country! Such frightening suppositions kept occurring to me. Finally I placed the whole matter in the Lord's hands. He would have to show me what was right.

By morning I had complete peace in my heart. At nine o'clock I climbed into the Land Rover and left the mission station. An hour later I was in Cox's Bazar. Situated on the coast of the Bay of Bengal, Cox's Bazar was headquarters for our subdivision, much like a county seat. It was the center for our local government and a beautiful place to enjoy the sandy ocean beach (more than seventy miles long—one of the longest beaches in the world). But today was not a day for enjoying the scenery!

I asked for and was given directions to the military headquarters. They had taken over a government rest house (like a motel) near the beach. At the gate I was halted abruptly by armed soldiers who demanded to know who I was, where I was going, and what my business was.

"I am a missionary from the hospital in Malumghat. I want to see the officer in charge," I told them.

I handed them my card, written in English on one side and Bengali on the other. Outwardly I was confident. Inside I was shaking. They eyed me suspiciously, then examined the card. (I was quite certain they couldn't read it anyway!) Then one soldier disappeared into the building, leaving the others to watch me.

Fifteen long, tense minutes passed. The young soldier finally returned and escorted me to the officer in charge. The officer sat guarded by several tommy-gun toting aides. He also had a pistol lying within reach. Sitting behind a tea-stained desk when I entered, the young, bright-looking officer rose to greet me politely. He motioned to a chair in front of the desk. At closer range, I could see he was a captain. He seemed to be very intelligent.

The captain tapped a desk bell, summoning a bearer, to bring tea and cookies. Then he began to ask inconsequential questions about the hospital and services rendered. After a few minutes, he shifted in his seat and asked how he could help me. With a prayer in my heart, I began.

"I am looking for the son of a very close friend. He is from a Buddhist family that lived near our mission station at Lama for many years. The father once helped me build a house, and I have watched his young son grow up to be a fine young man. The father reported that his son had been arrested about two weeks ago and brought to this place." I paused, watching the effect of my words. "I'm hoping to find out if he is well."

Again I paused. "His name is Robindra Barua."

The officer listened politely, but there was a definite change in his expression when I spoke the young man's name. "I don't know anyone here by that name. You have made a mistake."

I proceeded cautiously, knowing how tense the situation was. "Sir, I would be grateful to God if you could just double-check to see if Robindra is or isn't here. If he isn't, then I'll search elsewhere. If he is, I kindly request you to place him under my charge. I have known him and his family for ten years. I don't believe he is an enemy of Pakistan. I promise to be fully responsible."

Tea was served. The interview was over. I stood and shook the officer's hand. As I departed, I invited him to visit me at the hospital. I also informed him I would be sending Robindra's father to learn the results of his "double-check."

Shamakishor was anxiously waiting my return. I knew he would be there at the hospital compound, filled with hope and expectation. Sure enough, he was standing in the driveway; a loving father hoping for news of his son! As I drove past, I forced myself to smile in order to let him know there was still hope. Moments later, I shared with him what had transpired. "Come back in the morning," I told him. I assured him we would all be praying for his son.

Early the next morning, I typed an official letter to the captain, thanking him for the kind reception of the day before and introducing him to the bearer of the letter—Robindra's father. Shamakishor took the letter between trembling fingers and prepared to leave. He was very fearful. They might put him in prison too!

"Don't worry," I assured him. "God is able to do great things." The rest of the day I spent in prayer for him and for Robindra.

Two days later I was standing near the hospital entrance chatting with some patients. Suddenly I felt as though I were being tackled from behind. There were arms around my ankles. I struggled to maintain my balance. Looking down, I saw Shamakishor, his wife and their son Robindra before me, prostrate—touching their foreheads to my feet in humble gratitude. They were weeping. I will never forget the solemnity of that precious moment. I found myself weeping with that reunited family!

Shamakishor, his wife and Robindra Barua, "saved once"

Robindra's mother, wearing a soiled blue sari, rose to her knees and said through her tears, "Sahib, now I know why God sent you to Bangladesh. You have saved my son!"

Before the family left, I told them how God sent Jesus to rescue us from the clutches of sin. I told them how they could have true freedom in Christ. "This is the real reason I have come to Bangladesh," I said. "We want you to be free from sin and Satan!"

"Could one of the doctors examine Robindra?" Shamakishor asked, changing the subject. "He says there's no feeling in his left foot."

An examination was arranged. Dr. Donn Ketcham called me after a few minutes. It was then I learned the true story of Robindra's brush with death! The young prisoner had been repeatedly suspended in the air by his ankles! On one occasion it had been so long he thought his head would burst with the pressure of pulsating blood. The tight rope around his left ankle had cut off all circulation to that foot.

Dr. Ketcham prescribed certain massaging exercises for Robindra, feeling that nothing more could be done. And eventually Robindra's foot regained its circulation.

Four years later (1975) we were in the United States on furlough. A cassette tape was delivered with a message from missionary George Weber in Bangladesh. They were midway in their first term of service at the Hebron station. As a thoughtful gesture, they taped a report on what God was doing in the lives of many of our Bengali and tribal friends. There were so many names we recognized. In fact, the tape made us long to go back "home" to Bangladesh.

Midway through the tape, the voice of George came through, "Do you remember the carpenter in Bilchari Buddhist village—the one who worked for you? Well, their son Robindra has become a believer and is regularly attending our preaching services!"

Did I remember him? How could I ever forget? Saved once from death by my efforts, now he was saved eternally by Jesus Christ Himself!

10

ROBICHANDRO TIPPERAH
Evangelist with a vision

THEY HAD WALKED for several days through tangled jungles and over hazardous mountains. The exhausted men set up camp on our mission property and then came straight to me for help. This delegation of Tipperah tribesmen was plainly worried. Their spokesman was a thin young man with large, sad eyes. As he approached, he folded his hands and raised them to his forehead in a typical tribal greeting. "Nomoskar [hello]," he said. I returned the greeting. As I watched, he removed a short piece of hollow bamboo from his shoulder bag. From it he extracted a soiled piece of paper and offered it to me.

I carefully unrolled the scroll which had been written by a "professional writer"—a man in the marketplace who, for a small fee, writes letters for illiterate people. This petition bore the name of Robichandro Tipperah and had been clearly endorsed in one corner by his large thumbprint.

Robichandro, the young spokesman, watched my face as I read. The letter contained a request for a loan of 500 *takas* (approximately $100). He and his fellow villagers wanted the money for purchasing rice. I chatted with him a few minutes, then asked, "Why do you need such a large sum? That amount will buy hundreds of *seers* of rice!" (One *seer* is equal to two pounds.)

The man replied, "Sahib, there's a famine spreading throughout the hills. Children and some old people in my village have already died of starvation. We've exhausted our food supply. Unless we get help, all of us will die sooner or later."

Robichandro then related a most distressing story, which I later was able to confirm. Many other tribal people came with the same sad tale. Their rice crop had been destroyed by a plague of rats! Every seven years when the bamboo flowers, they explained, there is an overpopulation of rats. These greedy rodents, working feverishly throughout one night, can completely devastate a several-acre rice crop. They do such a thorough job that by morning not even a piece of straw is visible! I listened in amazement as Robichandro and his fellow villagers told how the cunning rats clip the rice stalks at ground level, then carry them away and hide them in holes so that nobody can trace their whereabouts.

There was a sincerity about Robichandro. (I later nicknamed him "Robi.") That evening I provided a hot meal for him and his party. While they ate rice and curry, we got better acquainted. Robi professed to be a Christian. He had accepted the Lord about a year before when evangelist Oncherai (see chapter 2) had preached in his village. It was evident, however, that he knew very little about the faith he now professed.

Long into the night I told them Bible stories from both the Old and New Testaments. Robi, whose perception seemed keener than the others', would translate my faltering Bengali into Tipperah so the other men could easily understand. I later learned that Robi was trilingual. Besides Tipperah, he could speak Bengali and Mogh.

The following morning, Robi and I discussed the proposed loan. I questioned, "How do you plan to repay the loan?"

Instead of answering, he handed me a soiled cloth tied into a bundle by its four corners. In it was wrapped silver bracelets, ear ornaments, and pounds of costly beads, which had been collected from the village women as a pawn for the urgently needed cash. I loaned him the money.

As I observed Robi, I realized he was a young man with true leadership ability. I invited him to attend our tribal Bible school to be held later on at Hebron. Before he departed for home, he promised he would make every effort to come.

Several weeks later, just before Christmas, he and several other men enrolled in our first annual short-term Bible school. I was thrilled to see Robichandro. That year ten young men sat under a week of concentrated Bible teaching. Robi's keen mind devoured everything we taught him. Long into the night, long after classes ended, it was thrilling to hear him retell the Bible stories.

When Bible school ended, Robi disappeared. Months passed, and we heard nothing from him. Then, one bazaar day, some visiting Tipperahs told me Robi lived near the Burma border; so I sent a message to him with those men.

A few days later he came to me, looking dejected and downhearted. We were sitting around an open fire in the yard when I brought up the matter about his loan. Ashamed and embarrassed, he said, "Sahib, I am unable to repay all of the money as I promised." However he did have a part of it and a story to explain the default.

As is so often true with the tribal peoples, he had been plagued with more misfortunes. His wife was seriously ill with what he thought was leprosy. That meant she would have to be ostracized from the main village. He was forced, according to tribal custom, to build another house some distance away from the village on a separate hillock.

This added expense was one he hadn't counted on. Then, too, he had reloaned some of the 500 *takas* to fellow villagers, several of whom couldn't pay him back. Robi had to suffer the loss. Purposely he had stayed away from me, chagrined that he couldn't pay all the loan on time.

I knew that Robi was telling the truth. After hearing his plausible story, I paid the balance of his debt and returned the jewelry. He was overjoyed, never expecting such grace. Tears of thankfulness appeared in his large, dark eyes. I shared more teaching from God's Word before he journeyed back to his village. "Leprosy can be cured," I assured him, and promised to make arrangements for his wife's treatment with our mission doctors.

Another tribal Bible school rolled around. Robi couldn't come. Instead he sent a message saying he had moved again to a new village. His elderly father was ill. Because of these developments, I didn't see Robi again before we went back to America on furlough.

Back from the States and two weeks into our second term, fellow missionary Harry Goehring died of kidney failure. He had been living at Hebron and was about to launch an extensive study of the Tipperah language. Before he got started, however, it pleased the Lord to take him Home. Once again we experienced a setback in our tribal work. Who would take Harry's place? Who would learn the Tipperah language? In time a Brooklyn, New York, pastor, Willard Benedict, learning of Harry's death and the need at Hebron, responded by coming to Bangladesh.

For the immediate future, however, the Field Council appointed me to carry on the tribal work from Malumghat, the location of the Memorial Christian Hospital. Hebron station would remain understaffed until the Benedicts could come from America. Living at Malumghat near the borders of tribal country, I began again to work with the Tipperah tribe.

When Robi learned I was back in Bangladesh, he searched for me. "Sahib, I've come with my family," he said. "They're at the hospital in one of the visitor's houses. Dr. Ketcham is going to examine my wife."

"How would you like to earn some money?" I asked. "You can work for me while you're staying here!" I assumed he would be around a long time if his wife was to be treated for leprosy.

Robi replied, "I'm not very strong and healthy, but I'll try. What do you want me to do?" He was thinking of physical labor.

I sat down and shared my burden with him. "I want so much to learn your Tipperah language. Since we both know Bengali, it should be quite easy. Will you help me?"

An expression of joy came over his face. "That will require months of time," he said. "Let me first return to my village and catch up the work. I'll come back after my rice is harvested in the fall."

When Robi was ready to leave for home, Dr. Ketcham had some good news. Robi's wife didn't have leprosy. She had been afflicted with a curable skin disease that made white blotches resembling leprosy. Medicines would take care of the illness.

Two months later Robi's rice crop was harvested, and he returned to be my language informant. While he had been away, his first son was born. He pointed proudly to the new baby and said, "I've named him *Walsh,* Sahib!" It had never occurred to me that one day I would have a namesake in the Tipperah tribe!

The following two years were very precious ones. Our lives became intertwined as Robi and I sought to unlock the mysteries of his mother tongue. I was soon engrossed in sentences with glottal stops and words with aspirates!

I used a simple English dictionary of the most common words needed to understand any language. Together we compiled a three-column dictionary of 2,500 words. The first column contained English words. The second had the Bengali equivalents. The last column—a labor of love—was in Tipperah. The Tipperah language has no written alphabet or script, so we used the Bengali alphabet to capture the Tipperah sounds.

This was exciting work! Next, we began to analyze the grammar. Missionary nurse Lynn Silvernale, with her linguistic training, joined to help me clear up some problems. A simple Tipperah grammar was the result!

At my urging, Robi moved his family from the interior to a Tipperah village nearer the hospital. I was convinced that a more regular access to them would also improve his work. He wouldn't worry so much if he could get home each weekend.

Robi's trips home became preaching opportunities too. He would go armed with flash cards and flannelgraph materials. On Monday mornings before I could begin language study, he would first have to share all the exciting news of his preaching feats on the weekend. Robi was indeed growing in the faith. He loved to preach!

Our furlough time rolled around again. Unemployed, Robi returned to the hills to earn his living. Once again it was a struggle to make a living. His whole family had suffered physically. However, when we returned to Bangladesh, I found him still firm in his faith. "I want to be an evangelist," he told me one afternoon. "God has given me a compelling burden to preach to the Mogh and Murung tribes."

The Mogh and Murung people inhabit those same hills to the east of the hospital where the Tipperahs live. Both tribal groups are totally unevangelized. After much deliberation, we missionaries felt led to hire Robi as a hospital-based evangelist to preach to tribal patients who came to be treated. A number of Mogh villages in close proximity to the hospital also needed to be reached for Christ. Robi began his ministry, making weekly trips to those villages.

The Moghs or Arakanese are of Burmese descent. They are devout followers of the Buddhist religion and are difficult to reach with the gospel. But they listened to Robichandro. His dynamic preaching captured their attention as nothing had in years. Soon he reported several converts. Dr. Vic Olsen also had a special burden for the Mogh people. On several occasions he and Robi would team up on evangelistic trips. Eventually their efforts paid off. A Mogh village chief and several men from one village were saved. A nucleus for an indigenous church was born!

In the fall of 1973 Robi's ministry widened. The Memorial Christian Hospital had obtained eighteen additional acres of jungle-covered land which had to be cleared. At my request, Robi spread the word in the hills that jungle-cutters were needed. Tribal people in Bangladesh spend their lives farming jungle-covered hills and mountains. Their "slash and burn" method of clearing land especially qualified them to do our work at the hospital station.

We had expected Tipperah people to respond to our offer for work, but instead a whole village of Murung tribesmen appeared! The Murungs are the most primitive of the tribal groups living in the hills along the Bangladesh-Burma border. Generally they avoid contact with outsiders. Their ethnic origins are still a mystery. They claim to be Buddhists, although it's a Buddhist religion mixed with spirit worship. Now the men and women of one whole village had responded to the call for work.

I hired these beautiful people to clear the jungle. What a sight it was! These simple menfolk, clad only in G-strings, wearing their long black hair tied in buns on the sides of their heads, began swinging their sharp machetes. Quickly they slashed the jungle to the ground. Their women and children, colorfully clad in home-woven cloth, worked beside them.

After work the men and boys would disappear into the nearby forests to hunt their evening meal: a dog, a tree lizard, or just jungle vegetation to be eaten with boiled rice. Their meal finished, they would squat around open fires, telling stories. Robi got their attention by taking out his flash cards. Then he would preach God's Word to them. I, too, often sat with them as Robi preached in a tongue I failed to understand. I observed in amazement as he captured his audience each evening with Bible stories!

The jungle-clearing job lasted several weeks. Toward the end of that time, Robi said, "Sahib, I have four new Murung believers. Would you allow them to give their testimonies before the church next Sunday morning?" Just like that!

My first reaction was to shout "Hallelujah!" But I quizzed Robi for more details. When were they saved? Are you sure they understand the gospel? Are they becoming Christians to get jobs? (This happens so often on the mission field that we tend to become very cautious.) But Robi convinced me these men were indeed born again!

Sunday morning before the message, opportunity was given to the four Murung believers to testify. Robi proudly led them to the front of the church, where each one spoke while Robi interpreted. That morning tears filled many eyes as we witnessed these first Murung believers boldly tell of their newfound faith in Christ.

A few days later, before a large crowd of Bengali and Tipperah Christians, the four men followed their Lord in believer's baptism. They were the firstfruits of Robi's efforts to reach the Murung people for Christ.

In a few days the number of converts grew to fifteen. The new ones expressed a desire to be baptized in a river near their own village. Now in complete control of the Murung work, Robi began making treks to their villages, preaching, baptizing, and teaching.

Our third term was drawing to a close. My wife, Eleanor, and I were busy packing in preparation for the trip home. Early on the final Saturday in Bangladesh, Robi came to me with a delegation of Murung Christians. As I opened the screen door, one man stepped forward and presented me with a large, live, red rooster! My first reaction was to question this sudden generosity. In Bangladesh nothing is given away absolutely free! There must be some "string" attached.

"What do they want?" I asked Robi, thinking of food, clothing, a loan, jobs.

Robi set my mind at rest. "These men want you to go to their village and dedicate their new 'Jesus-house.'" (Tribal people have no word for *church*.)

A new Jesus-house? In a Murung village? "You mean they've built a church in their village already?"

Robi nodded, his eyes shining. "Sahib, you must come and see it. They want you to be there for their first meeting."

Now I felt ashamed about judging their motives. We were extremely pressed for time, but I promised to go with them. My sense of being part of "history in the making" overruled other considerations, like helping my wife pack.

The following morning Robi and his Murung delegation were there to get me. We began our fourteen-mile trip early, walking steadily throughout the long, hot day. We came in sight of the village just as the sun was sinking low behind the westward mountains behind us.

The whole village was busy with activity. An advance man notified them we were coming. People were dashing here and there. "The missionary sahib is coming!" It was an exciting moment for me too!

The proud Murung believers led me straight to their Jesus-house. Like a sparkling diamond in a jeweled setting, the shiny new bamboo church was in the center of the Murung village. It was the most beautiful sight for this missionary to behold. The building reflected the last rays of the dying sun. The entryway had been decorated with clusters of wild flowers, including multicolored orchids! Robi, who had encouraged and help them build it, stood in the background like a proud father.

The Christians had prepared a feast of chicken curry and rice for me. We made preparation to have a dedication service in the new church after supper. Of the forty houses in the village, fifteen now professed faith in the Lord Jesus Christ. All of these new believers crowded into the building for that auspicious moment: the dedication of the first Murung church in the history of missions in Bangladesh!

On the morning of our departure for America, one of the original four Murung believers asked me to photograph him alone. I aimed my camera. "Wait!" he shouted. "I want a Bible to hold."

"Why? You can't read or write."

"Sahib," he pleaded, "I want to be a preacher too, like Robi. I want to learn all about what's in that Book!"

I placed a large Bengali Bible in his hand, backed off a little and lifted the camera to my face. My eyes found it difficult to focus as I viewed the scene before me: the Murung believer was caressing the Bible to his heart! The symbolism in that scene stirred me, and I was assured of the success of future Murung evangelism.

Dr. Vic Olsen took charge of Robi and the tribal evangelism work after our departure for the States. Under his guidance the work has continued to advance. Today there are at least eight Murung churches scattered throughout the hills, and a professing Christian population of several hundreds.

Robichandro, my Tipperah friend and brother in Christ, is still reaching the unreached for Christ in the Chittagong Hill Tracts of Bangladesh.

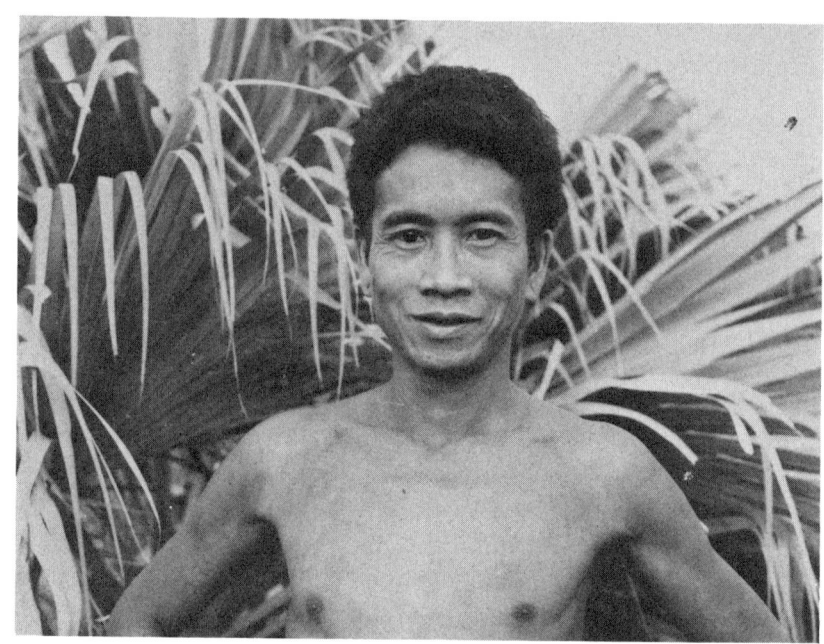

First Murung convert

Robi, baptizing one of first Murung converts

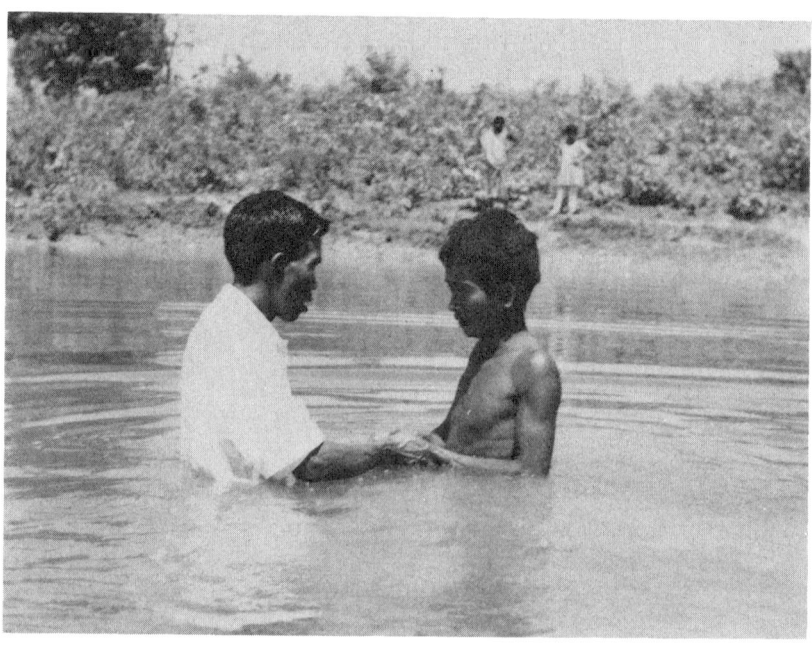

First Murung church; Robichandro and Murung believer

Robichandro Tipperah with Dr. Wendell Kempton, President of ABWE

11

PONINDRA LAL BARUA
Dry shrimp and chili peppers

I MET PONINDRA Lal Barua as he crossed the mission compound on his way to the hills. He was carrying a large basket at each end of his shoulder bar. Balanced on his tough shoulder muscles, the limber bar swayed gently as he moved along the path.

Ponindra was a very shy, introverted young fellow. He and his four brothers lived in a large, elongated mud house in the center of Bilchari Buddhist village. The five men were hard workers. Even though they lived near the mission compound, none of them had ever sought employment of the missionaries. However, they were friendly and talked with us when we would meet. Their strong devotion to their Buddhist religion and their higher standard of living enabled them to be more reserved toward us than their poorer neighbors.

Ponindra was one of the most timid men I'd ever met. On several occasions while I sat and chatted with the village men, I would notice him sitting alone in the shadows. He would look on and listen but never venture to join in the talk. The other men would laugh and ask questions, but Ponindra observed with no seeming interest to participate.

"Where are you going?" I asked him now as we met on the path.

Instead of answering, he lowered the bar from his shoulders and set down the baskets. This surprised me, because I expected him to keep on walking. Apparently Ponindra was going to break the silence barrier!

"I'm going to the Murung village," he responded. "I've got some business there."

I looked into his baskets. One was full of dry shrimp. Looking like pieces of reddish wood chips with heads and tentacles attached, they gave off a pungent odor that wasn't exactly appetizing. The other basket contained dry red chili peppers. Ground into a powder they add a spicy hot flavor to curry dishes. I have often eaten tribal curry. Sometimes it's so "chili hot" it is necessary to draw in cool air over the tongue before the next bite!

"You're going to sell these shrimp and peppers to the Murungs?" I asked. I realized how poor the tribal people were.

Ponindra shrugged his shoulders. "Sometimes I sell for cash. More often I trade for rice or cotton. Then I resell rice and cotton in the bazaar for a cash profit. This is the way I make my living, Sahib," he said.

This already was the most I had ever heard Ponindra say. Yet he still seemed in no hurry to go on his way. I said jokingly, "I wish I could go to the Murung villages with you. After you have completed your business, I could preach to the people about Jesus. Better yet, Ponindra, you could do both:

sell and *tell*. If you were a Christian, that would be a good job for you!"

Ponindra gave a feeble grin. "Sahib, I want to learn more about the Bible, but I am so busy. There just isn't time. I'm not happy in my religion because it doesn't give me any peace of mind."

He told me about his experience of becoming a Buddhist. "When I was about twelve, I was confirmed a Buddhist. Every boy in our village goes through this some time or another. This ceremony is called *moishung*. My head was clean-shaven, and I wore a saffron robe [the yellow-orange cloak identifying him with the priests]. I carried a walking stick, umbrella and begging bowl." (The begging bowl is a collection plate for daily gifts of food from the people. This is how the priests live.)

These items, plus a small hand fan, were all the worldly possessions a Buddhist *moishung* was permitted to have. These were necessary for completing the confirmation ceremony. At the end of nine days, Ponindra was pronounced a true believer of Buddha. During that time he was kept in the custody of veteran priests, learning how to meditate and deny himself earthly pleasures.

We talked for a few more minutes, then Ponindra picked up his yoke and said a parting good-bye. I watched him disappear into the hills, and was saddened that the yoke of sin on his heart was heavier than the shrimp and chili peppers he carried on his shoulders.

Shortly after this encounter, our family moved away from the Hebron station. I never returned there to live, although I have made periodic visits to the station since then.

Nine years later, on a visit to Hebron, I again met Ponindra walking alone on a village trail one evening. A full moon hung silently in the sky, helping me to recognize him.

"*Nomoskar*, Ponindra," I said, using the typical greeting.

He seemed genuinely happy to see me. For more than an hour we stood under a beautiful full moon talking about spiritual things. He had just left his brother-in-law Shudhir's house (see chapter 3) where they had been talking about the missionaries. Ten years before Shudhir had been the first man from the Bilchari village to accept the Lord. Now it was evident that Ponindra, too, wanted to learn more about Jesus.

"We've just been talking about you, Sahib," he said.

"Oh, really? And what were you saying?" I asked. One of

the favorite pasttimes of the nationals seems to be to talk about the foreigners in their midst.

Ponindra said, "We think you ought to move back to Hebron and live near us. We feel more secure with your presence in the village."

Ponindra, like others of the Buddhist village, was expressing a concept he couldn't fully understand. Why did he feel more secure when we missionaries were present on the station? Perhaps there was a prestige factor that inflated their egos. Or they might feel physically safer from the threat of bandits who roam the countryside. These are possible reasons. But the real one, which Ponindra couldn't express, was obvious. We were standing for the truth. As God-fearing people, we provided the "salt of the earth" for that area.

I thanked Ponindra for the compliment, but said, "You want me to come back, but when I lived here before, you never attended any of my Bible classes. In fact, you never even came to my house to visit!"

He acted very embarrassed and stammered, "I'm sorry, Sahib. I do have a strong desire to learn more about Christianity though. Shudhir has been telling me a lot about Christ. Could you get me a Bible of my own?"

This time I sensed that Ponindra was not just chatting to be polite. I promised to honor his request after I returned to the hospital station where I lived.

A week later, I dispatched a runner to carry a packet of literature to Ponindra. In it was a copy of the Gospel of Luke, plus some assorted Christian tracts and booklets. I enclosed a note encouraging him to meet with missionary Willard Benedict, who was now in charge of the Hebron mission station.

As 1970 ended, Bangladesh experienced the world's greatest natural calamity. A devastating cyclone smashed into the coastal areas of the Bay of Bengal, killing a half-million people in one night! Then, the next year, the Bengali people revolted against their non-Bengali masters. Civil war broke out, leaving thousands homeless and destitute.

Ponindra's village suffered, as did most of the Hindu and Buddhist villages throughout the land. Their homes were searched by pro-military *goondas* (thugs). In many cases the people stood helplessly by as their homes were stripped of valuable possessions.

Ponindra recalls those terrible days when his country was

at war. "After you sent me that packet of Christian books, I read a few of them. But I ended up hiding them in the rafters of the house. I didn't want anyone to know I was interested in Christianity. Then the war came bringing so much misery. I was upset in my heart. My brother-in-law Shudhir died suddenly, and I was torn up in despair. I watched his Christian friends bury him on the mission compound. All these events came crushing in on me, causing me to remember the hidden books in the rafters! I got them down and began to read."

When Ponindra read the Gospel of Luke, his heart softened. "For the Son of man is come to seek and to save that which was lost" (19:10). "Why seek ye the living among the dead? . . . Then he said unto them, O fools, and slow of heart to believe all that the prophets have spoken" (24:5, 25). The powerful Sword of the Spirit was doing its work in his heart.

One restless night he had a dream that literally changed his life. It spurred him into action. "In my dream," he recalls, "I saw an old man walking toward me. Three times he asked me if I believed what I had been reading in the Bible. On the third time, I said, 'Yes, I believe.' Then the old man said, 'If you truly believe with all your heart, go tell Benedict Sahib and the other missionaries.'"

Ponindra said he awoke with a start. He prayed a simple prayer as beads of sweat poured from his body: "Lord, I believe! Save me!"

He felt God's peace come over him, but he could not sleep. The missionaries might rejoice over his conversion, but certainly his friends and neighbors would not! It would be problem enough to approach the missionaries because of his shyness! How could he go to the missionary? He had never even met him. For the rest of the night he tossed in fear. What would happen now?

The fear reaction is justifiable. To renounce one's religion for Christianity often means severe physical persecution (see chapter 6), loss of inheritance, and sometimes the loss of one's wife.

In the morning, however, in spite of his fears, Ponindra went to see Willard Benedict to share the news of his conversion. "I had never even met Benedict Sahib. I knew he would wonder why I was coming to him."

Willard greeted him warmly, but questioned him carefully. "Do you need a job? Do you need money?"

Missionaries know from experience that many people will profess to be Christians just to get financial help. They are known as "rice Christians." Willard wanted to be sure Ponindra's motives were pure.

"I don't need a job, and I don't need money," Ponindra told Willard. "I have lived here all my life. In the eleven-year history of your mission station, I have never once come seeking for work."

Willard believed that Ponindra's testimony was genuine. After hearing every detail, they prayed and rejoiced together. Then he made arrangements for Ponindra to receive regular Bible teaching on a one-to-one basis.

"It's been a thrill to see Ponindra's faith develop," Willard reported to me later. "He attends every service and drinks in the Word of God like a thirsty soul!"

But until December 1976 Ponindra wasn't ready to be baptized. He had lived in fear of reprisals from his influential family. He once told me that if he were baptized his father-in-law would take his wife away from him. Finally when he became convinced that he must make a clear-cut testimony of his faith to the people, he asked missionary Dave Totman for baptism. Dave and Doris Totman had since replaced the Benedicts who returned to America.

Dave spent several weeks giving Ponindra special teaching about baptism and Christian living. Then one day a real test came, and Dave was convinced that Ponindra was indeed a born-again Christian.

Each year after the long monsoon season ends, the village people are expected to repair the Buddhist temple. This particular year the bamboo fence needed replacing. Each family in the village was assigned the responsibility of doing a certain section at their own expense. Ponindra's family was also assigned a section of fence!

Ponindra and Dave walked past the temple area together. Pointing to a large gap in the newly installed fence, Ponindra said proudly, "I refused to build my section, Sahib. Now they know I really am a Christian!"

Several days after Ponindra was baptized, he was kidnapped from his home. His hysterical wife came crying to Dave with the news. In the middle of the night, someone kept calling Ponindra's name. He thought he recognized the voice, so he opened the door. Several men grabbed him and dragged him to the edge of the river. There they threatened to beat him if he didn't renounce his Christian faith.

He refused to recant. He was beaten and taken several miles away to a place deep in the jungle. His kidnappers couldn't decide whether or not to kill him. Then one man appeared who talked them out of it. "Shoot me instead," the stranger offered.

The kidnappers were momentarily diverted from their evil scheme. But they were not about to release Ponindra. Instead they came up with a new idea. "Let's demand one thousand *takas* [equivalent to $90 at that time] ransom. Surely the missionary will pay us to get the Christian back!"

A ransom note was sent to Dave. Dave and I were concerned about Ponindra, but after talking it over, we decided not to send any ransom money. We would commit Ponindra to God's care and keeping. To pay the kidnappers would be to establish a precedent. Every convert from then on might be kidnapped for a ransom.

Two days later Ponindra, shaken but unharmed, returned to the mission compound. His captors, all devout Buddhists, decided their tactics were futile. Ponindra's life had been spared, and he had not denied his Lord.

Slowly, very slowly, the work of God goes on in the garden of Buddha. With men like Ponindra coming to the truth, there will one day be a strong indigenous church in Bilchari Buddhist village.

12

DEBAPRIYA ROY
Out of the maze, into the light

"HE'S WAKING NOW," he heard someone say.

His drugged, half-conscious mind just wouldn't bring things into focus. The room seemed to go in circles when he tried to open his eyes. It was something like the experience he had as a child at the *Bohu Chakra* ceremonies he had attended in the village. An elaborate maze was constructed in front of the temple. Only one route through it led to the statue of Buddha. There were lines of circular bamboo entrances to the maze. At the blow of a whistle, all the village children would run into the maze. The first one reaching the Buddha without running into an obstruction was considered to be righteous and good. How Debapriya wanted to reach the statue and come into the light!

Suddenly his brain cleared, and he became aware that he was in a hospital. "Untie my feet and let me go home!" he demanded angrily. But no one was touching his feet. His legs felt heavy and useless, as though weighted down by stones.

"What does he mean?" a frightened voice asked. That was his father's voice.

Nurses and doctors moved in and out of the room, anxious to assure the conscious patient that he was going to be all right. This patient was very important . . . this nineteen-year-old boy who had been thrown from his motorcycle.

"He'll be all right," he heard the doctor explain to his mother. "The X rays were perfectly normal. It will just be a matter of time before he'll be up and around."

Debapriya Roy was not an ordinary patient. His cousin was the king, and he had been raised in an atmosphere of wealth and luxury. Anything he wanted he could get—including the Kawasaki motorcycle he insisted he must have!

After he graduated from high school, he had wanted to join the Bangladesh army. But his mother had her heart set on an engineering career for her very special firstborn son. His mind was set on a military life. He left home and went to Dacca, where he met the prime minister of Bangladesh, Sheikh Mujibur Rahman, a personal friend of the Roy family. The chief army commander urged him to join the service, promising him a commission as an officer.

His mother's letters urged him to return home and take up engineering. So he returned for a time, listening to the arguments against his choice of a career. Finally Debapriya said, "Okay. I'll go into engineering if you'll buy me a new motorcycle." He had been begging them for one for several years. Reluctantly they agreed. Now they were all sorry!

About 5:20 on January 16, 1975, Debapriya and two of his best friends stepped out of a restaurant near his home in Rangamati. He jumped on his brand-new Kawasaki motorcycle, but for some unexplainable reason it refused to start. His friends would push him, they said. He was angry and embarrassed that a new cycle wouldn't start, so he raced the engine and roared off in frustration when it finally got going. His two buddies jumped on, and they headed down the hill as other friends watched enviously.

Down, down the hill they went. They then spotted a man sitting in the middle of the road. Debapriya sounded his horn and slowed down. The man slowly rose to his feet, moved to one side, but continued to walk down the road with his back to the oncoming cycle. Debapriya, still upset, accelerated again. Just as he started to pass the pedestrian, the old man darted across the road in front of him. The cycle grazed the man, causing Debapriya to lose control.

The two riders fell off as the cycle careened down the hill, finally throwing Debapriya off onto his back. It wasn't until 2:30 the next morning that he regained consciousness in a Rangamati hospital. In a matter of minutes he had plunged from happiness to despair. Now his parents realized (and eventually he also knew) that he was paralyzed from the waist down.

With enough money and influence, everything would be done that could be for their son. Debapriya's father was a wealthy landowner and fruit farmer, raising mangoes, jackfruit, pineapples and bananas. His mother, though a homemaker, was of royal descent. His grandmother serves as an advisor to the president of Bangladesh in the areas of relief and rehabilitation.

Debapriya *must* get better. As the oldest son in such a prominent family so much was expected of him. The Roy family belonged to the royal Chakma family who ruled over the middle third of the territory in the Chittagong Hill Tracts district. (The Chittagong Hill Tracts is the border district in Bangladesh that stretches from Assam, India, to Burma. The area is inhabited by a number of tribal ethnic groups, one of the largest of which is the Chakma tribe, numbering 450,000 people. The Chittagong Hill Tracts district is divided into thirds, with a tribal king administering each subdivision.) Debapriya's cousin is the present reigning king. They grew up together in the capital town of Rangamati, enjoying privileges that only the wealthy could have.

The doctors in the hospital said Debapriya would improve. But as time went by, he began running a low fever and losing weight. Six days after the accident, his family transferred him to the Medical College in Chittagong, fifty miles away.

"I was terribly depressed," the young man recalls. "I couldn't understand why it was taking me so long to get over a motorcycle accident."

The doctors at the Chittagong hospital ordered a new series of X rays. Again the reports came back: normal. This time the doctors prescribed a hard bed for him, feeling that perhaps the nerve problem would resolve itself if the patient used a hard bed.

Twenty-two days later his condition was worse. His fever wouldn't subside. The troubled family began to discuss other plans. Maybe they would take him to India where they could have the choice of a number of famous hospitals. They considered the problem involved in transporting him and decided to try for help in Dacca, the capital of Bangladesh. They heard of an American doctor of some fame who worked in a leading government hospital in that city.

Babul Absar, Debapriya's closest friend (one who had been riding with him on that fateful day), was sent by the family to contact the doctor in Dacca. Two days later he returned with bad news. Babul had been told that Debapriya probably had a spinal injury which would require specialists in neurosurgery. The hospital at Dacca was not equipped to handle such cases. But Babul also came back with a ray of hope. While he was in Dacca, he spent a night with friends at the Dacca University. One of them, hearing Debapriya's story, told about the Memorial Christian Hospital at Malumghat.

Babul had never heard of the place. But the friend said, "I was playing soccer there a couple years ago and seriously fractured my leg. A very special doctor called Dr. Olsen cared for me. My leg is as good as new now!"

Debapriya's parents, too, had never heard of the hospital. They didn't know of Dr. Olsen or even the area of Malumghat. They located it on a map and set out the next morning to find it, sixty-five miles away. Four hours later their small motor rickshaw pulled into the hospital entrance. Dr. Olsen was called. After a few minutes of discussion, an appointment was made to bring the injured young man the next day.

"I'll never forget that day," Debapriya said. "The date is etched in my memory. It was February 11, 1975. We arrived at the hospital about 5:15, after an agonizing trip over the rough roads. Sister Millie [missionary nurse Mildred Cooley] received me with a smiling face and admitted me to the best room in the hospital, the one reserved for the missionaries when they are sick. She made me feel very comfortable." Debapriya also remembered the tall American doctor who arrived a short time later and took a history of the case. He ordered more X rays the following morning.

The next day, after a careful study of the X rays, Dr. Olsen's suspicions were confirmed. The spinal cord was certainly damaged. For the first time the problem was pinpointed. No one before—with all the X rays taken—had been able to diagnose the case accurately.

After a weekend of thinking and praying about the situation, Dr. Olsen decided to put his handsome young patient in traction. A very serious, specialized operation would have to be performed on the young man with the severed spinal cord.

"I was wheeled into the operating room," Debapriya remembers. "When all the medical people gathered around my bed, Dr. Olsen started praying." This was the first prayer he had ever heard. It left an indelible impression on his wondering mind.

The next ten weeks were misery for him as he lay helpless in bed. His body was stretched from both ends. He had plenty of time to think. Over and over he said, "If only I hadn't demanded that motorcycle!"

The afternoon of that last ride kept coming to his mind. His mother and he had purchased plane tickets for a pleasure trip to India on January 17th. His friends wanted him to go to an afternoon movie with them. "You'll be leaving tomorrow for India, and we won't see you for a few weeks," they said.

"No," Debapriya told them. "I've already seen that movie. I'll just ride around on my cycle and wait until the movie is over."

Here in the hospital at Malumghat a depression settled down on him. But the testimony of the Christian staff at

Memorial Christian Hospital was beginning to have its effect. The visits of Dr. Olsen, Dr. DeCook, physiotherapist Larry Golin and the nurses impressed him. These were the very finest Christians he had ever met. They were gentle and kind, often taking time to pray or read the Bible with him.

Debapriya got to the place he wished he could end his life. Then one afternoon, in this frame of mind, he looked down at his younger sister who was sitting on the floor beside his bed. She had picked up the Bible from the stand and was reading it. Debapriya also started to read the Bible. Suddenly some words seemed to jump out at him. "Come unto me, all ye that labour and are heavy laden, and I will give you rest. Take my yoke upon you, and learn of me; for I am meek and lowly in heart: and ye shall find rest unto your souls" (Matt. 11:28,29).

"As I read those lines," Debapriya told me later, "the great depression lifted. I felt a strange and unexplainable peace come over me."

Debapriya, like the rest of the Chakma people, had been raised a Buddhist. He remembers going to the temple with offerings for the bronze Buddha. His fondest memories had been of the special holy days which were celebrated annually. One called *Bohu Chakra* (many circles) was a day when the people constructed a maze in front of the god-statue. How he wanted to be the winner of that race to the statue. But peace and righteousness always eluded him. His life had been one blind alley after another.

Because of family wealth perhaps, Debapriya never took his religion very seriously. He considered himself a "young tough." He needed nothing . . . no deity. He was full of youthful pride. But all was changed now. Lying on the hospital bed in Memorial Christian Hospital, he was confronted with the realities of God and of God's demand on his life. He began to read the Scriptures daily. Slowly his defenses crumbled, his hardened heart softened, his pride yielded. God's Word was doing its work.

These verses hammered at him: "As it is written, There is none righteous, no, not one. . . . For all have sinned, and come short of the glory of God" (Rom. 3:10, 23). "Knowing that a man is not justified by the works of the law, but by the faith of Jesus Christ . . ." (Gal. 2:16).

On May 30 when Dr. Olsen made his rounds, a misty-eyed Debapriya told the doctor that he wanted to become a Christian. In the quiet of the hospital room he yielded his life to the Lord. His struggle for inner peace and forgiveness was over.

Slowly, very slowly, as Larry Golin patiently worked with him, Debapriya began to wiggle his toes! Feeling returned to his lower extremities. His headaches ceased. Soon he was moving about in a wheelchair. His broad smile conveyed the joy in his heart.

He continued to grow in the Lord, and one day he asked the pastor to baptize him. With the doctor's permission, it was arranged. On December 12, before a large crowd, including his Buddhist relatives, he was immersed, sitting in his wheelchair!

Two days before my baptism," Debapriya revealed later, "Satan did his best to change my mind. It was as if this was his last chance at my life. Doubts flooded my soul, and my head began to ache as it had done before I was saved. Satan kept saying, 'Wait, wait. Do it later!' "

In that final struggle he turned to the Lord and said; "Lord, give me the strength to go through with this baptism, even if I have to die!"

Since that time Debapriya has progressed physically to the point that he can now walk short distances with the help of braces. His daily travels (via wheelchair) take him from his quarters on the corner of the compound to the hospital laboratory where he has been receiving training as a laboratory technician.

More recently (November 1977), Debapriya and I attended a Bible translation seminar in the capital city of Dacca. During that week Debapriya not only learned the skills of translation methodology, he also became excited about the prospects of translating God's Word in his own Chakma language.

The only believer in the Chakma tribe, Debapriya has his future challenge clearly before him. He wants to help his people medically and spiritually. "My goal is to return to Rangamati and serve my people," he says with confidence. "I know of no better way than to set up a good medical clinic where I can help people both physically and spiritually as I have been helped. All my people must hear the good news of eternal life in Jesus Christ."

No more blind alleys for Debapriya! He is out of the maze of sin and hopelessness and into the light of the Lord Jesus Christ!

EPILOGUE

THE STORIES YOU have just read are about real people . . . people like yourself. In no way are we to consider these dear saints of God as "super saints." They, too, are made of flesh and blood. Satan is their adversary. They all struggle with the world, the flesh, and the devil just as we do. In fact, their struggle against the forces of evil may be even greater than ours from several points of view.

Poverty. Bangladesh is the poorest nation on earth. The average annual per capita income, based on the gross national product, is less than $65 per year!

Her 84 million people are crowded into the land at an average of more than 1,400 people per square mile. And the population continues to increase.

Quite naturally the struggle to survive occupies the minds of most people, including the Christians. Satan uses poverty to detract Christians from spiritual pursuits. Because of the "cares of this world," the Word of God is not allowed to take root and bear fruit as it should.

Illiteracy. It is estimated that 80 percent of the people in Bangladesh cannot read or write. In order to make it possible for the populace to vote, each political party chooses its own symbol. This may be anything from an umbrella to an ox cart. On voting day, the illiterate simply put a mark under the symbol which represents the person or party of their choice.

From the spiritual point of view, the illiterate suffer greatly. They are unable to read the Word of God and edifying Christian literature. Satan again finds such people to be ready prey. Instead of finding scriptural solutions to their problems, they often revert to their pagan practices or lean on human wisdom. As a result the church suffers.

Persecution. When a person becomes a Christian he is usually ostracized by his family. More often than not, he becomes the object of disdain and persecution. We have known many who have suffered for their Christian faith. (See chapters

6 and 11.) The persecution is usually instigated by relatives and always supported by the religious community.

Satan uses fear as a weapon to discourage people from making a decision for Christ. Fear is also a weapon to hold in check those who have already believed but want to advance in the faith.

When we consider the numerous problems faced by believers in foreign lands, it should challenge us to pray, upholding them before the throne of God. The apostle Paul advised: "I exhort therefore, that, first of all, supplications, prayers, intercessions, and giving of thanks, be made for all men" (1 Tim. 2:1). The "all men" includes our beloved brethren in other lands around the globe, including Bangladesh.

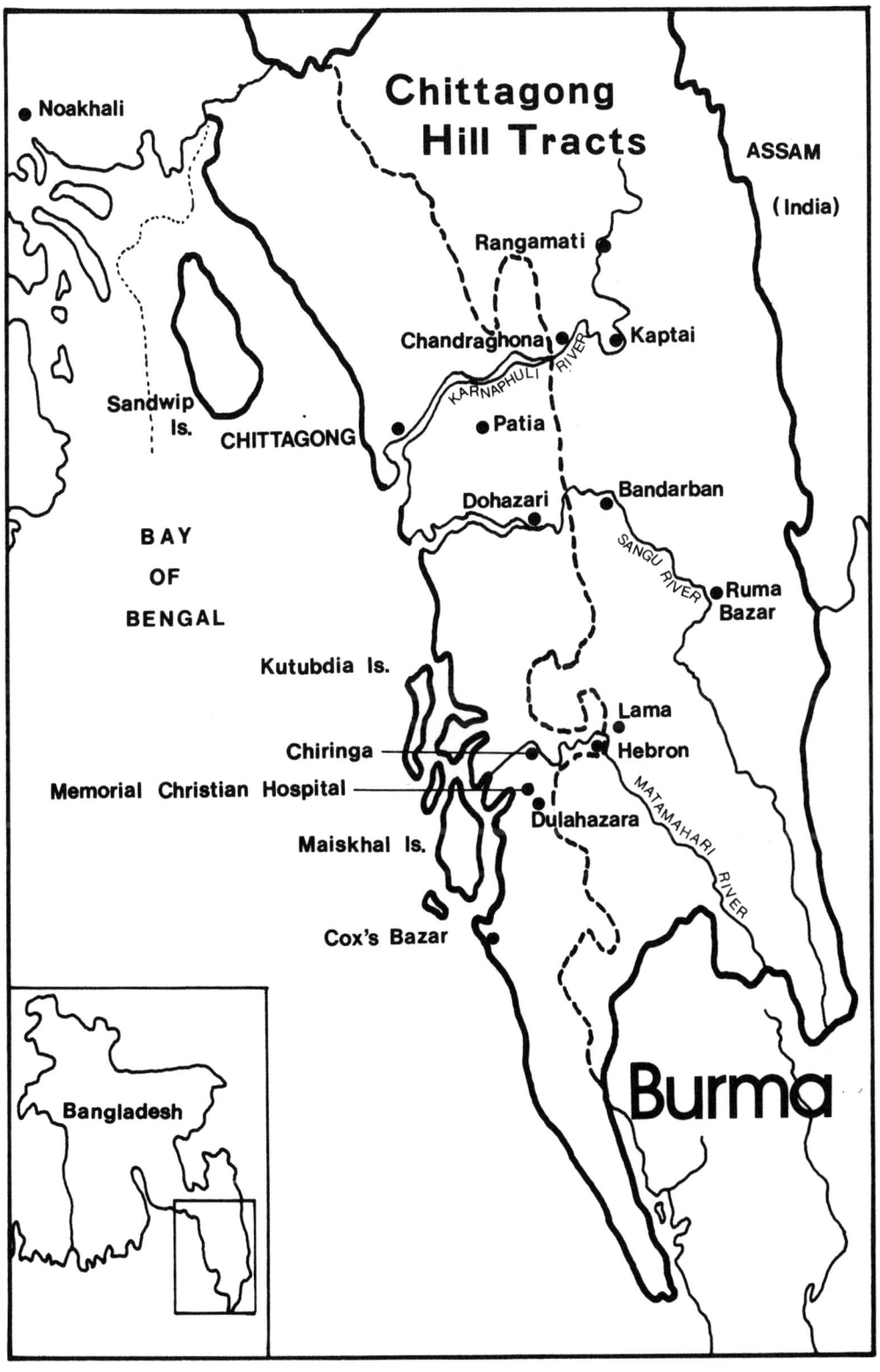